T0209943

LIVING

F O R

POSTERITY

My Remarkable African Mother
Bo Wabei Lisulo, a.k.a. Bo Ma-Matauka

Sibeso Mukoboto Luswata, Ed.D

WESTBOW
PRESS®
A DIVISION OF THOMAS NELSON
& ZONDERVAN

WestBow Press books may be ordered through booksellers or by contacting:

WestBow Press
A Division of Thomas Nelson & Zondervan
1663 Liberty Drive
Bloomington, IN 47403
www.westbowpress.com
844-714-3454

ISBN: 979-8-3850-1053-0 (sc)
ISBN: 979-8-3850-2109-3 (hc)
ISBN: 979-8-3850-1054-7 (e)

Library of Congress Control Number: 2023920057

Print information available on the last page.

WestBow Press rev. date: 03/05/2024

Bo Ma-Matauka

To the memory of an incredible mother,
Bo Wabei Lisulo, a.k.a. Bo Ma-Matauka
In loving memory of our father, Daniel Fwanyanga
Mukoboto, who dreamed all the dreams that our
mother prayed through to their realization

Daniel Fwanyanga Mukoboto

In loving memory of our dear uncle, our mother's brother, Mr. Daniel Muchiwa Lisulo, who stood by our mother through all those years until he passed away in August 2000. They were the best of friends, and through their friendship, we learned much about God and how to best navigate life. He encouraged and supported our mother and all of us in realizing our father's dreams.

In rememberance of my dearest friend of more than thirty-five years, Auntie Dr. Mbololwa Mbikusita-Lewanika, heavenly royalty who went to be with the Lord in 2020. Part of me felt ripped off at her passing on. In her lifetime, Auntie Mbololwa held my hand, lifted me up, walked alongside me as a destiny helper in pursuit of my dreams and my growth as a Christian. Isaiah 54 remained our reference point for life. I shall always cherish the special relationship I enjoyed with Auntie Mbololwa as a family member, friend, and sister in Christ until that day when we shall meet again.

CONTENTS

Foreword xi

Preface xiii

Acknowledgements xvii

Chapter 1   A Historical Background 1

Chapter 2   Bo Ma-Matauka: The Church Planter 22

Chapter 3   A Rich Legacy by Bo Wabei Lisulo,
a.k.a. Bo Ma-Matauka 27

Chapter 4   Meet Bo Wabei Lisulo, a.k.a. Bo Ma-Matauka 32

Chapter 5   Lessons from My Mother 40

Chapter 6   Faith, Hope, and Love 57

Chapter 7   The Key of Obedience 69

Chapter 8   My Mother's Homegoing 74

Chapter 9   My Mother's Blessing 86

Chapter 10   The Generational Impact 93

Chapter 11   Bo Ma-Matauka Posterity 107

Afterword 111

Selected Bibliography 115

FOREWORD

I am honored and delighted to write this foreword for a remarkable testimony of a transformative leader, written by my friend and sister, Dr. Sibeso Luswata. I have read the book in awe of the incredible "Mother of Many," the author's beloved mother, Bo Wabei Lisulo. On the other hand, I am not so surprised about Bo Wabei Lisulo's remarkable courage, faith, love, heart of service, and spirit of excellence because it is exactly what I have experienced in the past fourteen years I have known her daughter, Dr. Sibeso. She is a dear friend, partner in ministry as continental leaders of the BEZA International Christian Fellowship, colleague, and leader at the United Nations.

As leaders of the BEZA International Christian Fellowship and contributors to the Africa Arise movement, we co-authored a series of four books, together with other members of the Fellowship, namely *The Kingdom of God Will Never Be Shaken* (2011), *Church Arise and Redeem the Nations in Righteousness in this Season of Jubilee* (2012), *Walking in Destiny and Purpose* (2013), and *Redeeming Zambia in Righteousness* (2015). The last series was prepared in partnership with Bishop Joshua Banda, leader of the Assemblies of God, Eastern and Southern Africa; the late Dr. Roland Msiska (former Secretary to the Cabinet in Zambia and my mentor), and other key partners in Zambia.

This book you are reading, *Living for Posterity—My Remarkable African Mother: Bo Wabei Lusulo a.k.a. Bo Ma-Matauka*, has inspired me immensely. It has given me a clear understanding of the importance of intergenerational impact and that whatever we do in this generation is a seed sown to multiply in future generations. We must indeed plant good seeds in good soil.

It has taught me that a deep love for God and His Word propels one into service to others with effortless but genuine love. It drives purpose, shapes dreams, and empowers people with energy and resources to serve the most vulnerable while influencing decisions that affect their lives.

I have also learned that God's miracles are still alive in our days! The way he shut the mouths of lions in the story of Daniel in Babylon is the same way he shut the mouth of the lion Bo Wabei Lisulo encountered in the rolling hills of Zambia, with my friend Sibeso as a child strapped on her back! The Lord spared His daughters for a great purpose. Sibeso, in her capacity as chief of education in UNICEF and expert in other platforms, has shaped education policies and practices globally and particularly in Africa. As a Christian minister, she has diligently mentored the Young African Thinkers in Ethiopia, Zambia, and Kenya. She has touched numerous lives with her love and generosity. She has also taught me what it means to be a true servant and friend of God. This is a book of inspiration and hope for all who read it.

Christine Musisi, resident representative of UNDP Tanzania (2019–2023) and founder of ONGOZA Africa!

PREFACE

The Lion Encounter

Painting of a lion in the savannah.

In the rolling hills of Zambia, between Mongu and Lukulu, a mother with one baby strapped on her back and another's hand firmly tucked in hers walked behind an escort guide team through the African savannah. At that time, wild animals, including lions, were a common sight as they roamed the plains, camouflaged behind bushes and forest trees, waiting for prey. Bo Wabei Lisulo, a.k.a. Bo Ma-Matauka, and her escort team came across a ferocious lion. Upon seeing the lion, the petrified armed escort fled with their weapons, leaving her and her two little children to face the king of the jungle in a one-on-one confrontation to either save herself and her children or perish.

Extremely frightened, she was completely aware of the grave danger she was in. She could not run or leave her children behind. She had apparently reached the end of her rope. My mother did the only thing she knew as a remedy for desperate times such as the one she was in: she prayed deep groans, the kind of supplications that words could never describe. Keeping her eyes straight on the beast and with trembling hands, she unstrapped her baby from the back and positioned her and the other young daughter to her front in a bid to protect them. She earnestly prayed and called on the Lion of Judah to shut the mouth of the lion before her. She recalled a story the missionary in her village had shared of a man called Daniel, who had survived the den of lions in ancient days. Something inside her was so strong that this was still possible in her day.

Indeed, the Lion of Judah shut the mouth of this lion in the jungle, for as though under some instruction or beckoning, the maned lion simply turned away and disappeared into the African savannah. Our mother lived to tell the story of her determination to protect her children at all costs, but especially about a God who is a mighty deliverer. Years later, she told of the courage in fear that enabled her to risk being devoured by the lion, simply because she was convinced that her two daughters had a destiny and needed her protection. She believed that even if she had died, her two girls would somehow have been saved. She believed someone would have come from the nearby village where they had spent the night, would somehow know her father, and would have taken them home to safety.

She often said she knew deep inside that it was not their time to die. Years later and true to her convictions, these two daughters did grow up into strong women who have sat in global platforms gatherings and have had a voice in continental meetings held in the heart of Africa, working for the world as their earthly father had envisioned. These two daughters stand today as witnesses that God rescued them from the lion encounter for a mission and have taken the time to write this book in memory of their remarkable mother.

Bo Ma-Matauka prayed in the spirit because this is what she had been taught while learning under some missionaries at Sefula when revival hit the land in 1934–1935. That was the year when Litunga (King) Yeta 111 (Lewanika) declared Bulozi a Christian nation and placed the Ebenezer stone at Sefula in 1935, symbolizing the jubilee and founding of the PEMS church in Bulozi. Bo Ma-Matauka, our mother, believed in the power of praying in the spirit, as she remembered the Word in Romans 8:26–27 (NLT).

> And the Holy Spirit helps us in our weakness. For example, we don't know what God wants us to pray for. But the Holy Spirit prays for us with groanings that cannot be expressed in words. And the Father who knows all hearts knows what the Spirit is saying, for the Spirit pleads for us believers in harmony with God's own will.

Was she afraid? Many would ask her. Very afraid, as she would later say, but she had to do it afraid. As she prayed in the spirit, the lion simply turned and majestically walked away, leaving her a nervous wreck with her daughters unharmed. She proceeded on her journey to find the armed escort guides who had deserted her and her children. They were flabbergasted at seeing her arriving safe and sound and wondered aloud how that could be. They had naturally expected that the lion had feasted on this poor woman and her children for dinner that day, but here she was with her two daughters, unscathed. *How did she survive that lion encounter? What kind of a woman was this?!* they wondered in amazement.

This book is written in honor of this remarkable African woman, a courageous mother, with the sole purpose of honoring God who makes all things possible. This book is about the rich, godly, unperishable inheritance that has been passed on to us, an inheritance stored in heaven for generations to come. Our mother taught us to completely depend on God as our Father and provider. "I led Israel along with my ropes of kindness and love. I lifted the yoke from his neck, and I stooped to feed him" (Hosea 11:4 NLT).

She also reminded us constantly that God's promise was to never forget or leave us. "Never! Can a mother forget her nursing child? Can she feel no love for the child she has borne? But even if that were possible, I would not forget you!" (Isaiah 49:15 NLT).

Herein is a story of courage, determination, and purpose, detailing valuable lessons that our mother, Bo Wabei Lisulo (Bo Ma-Matauka), lived out and taught us during her ninety-two years of life. Herein is the story of a remarkable woman with a rich legacy of love for her family, her community, and all people. She understood the value of shaping and protecting the destiny of generations after her. Therefore, we have also set our hearts on elements that

> We will not hide these truths from our children; we will tell the next generation about the glorious deeds of the Lord, about his power and his mighty wonders. For he issued his laws to Jacob; he gave his instructions to Israel. He commanded our ancestors to teach them to their children, so the next generation might know them—even the children not yet born—and they in turn will teach their own children. So each generation should set its hope anew on God, not forgetting his glorious miracles and obeying his commands. (Psalms 78:4–7 NLT)

ACKNOWLEDGEMENTS

Glory to God who makes all things possible!

Acknowledgments go to:

- Northmead Assembly of God Church in Lusaka, Zambia
- Bishop Joshua HK Banda and Pastor Mrs. Gladys ZM Banda
- Reverend Frazier and Mrs. Jean Khatanga
- Reverend Raymond and Mrs. Matilda Nyirenda
- Pastor Haggai and Mrs. Mweene and all the church leaders and church members who prayed
- The Africa Arise Movement
- Dr. Betta Mengistu
- Pastor Mrs. Sophie Mengistu
- Pastor Zerubbabel Mengistu
- Pastor Sahle Shiferaw
- BEZA International Ministries in Ethiopia
- The International Christian Fellowship (ICF) at BEZA
- The Young African Thinkers
- All the brethren at Watoto Ministries in Uganda, Christ is the Answer Ministries (CITAM) in Nairobi, Kenya, Hatfield Christian Centre (HCC) in Pretoria, and VUKA Africa in South Africa and Botswana
- Those who stood with us in continuous prayer and offered words of encouragement during this project

Lilian Njoki Kasanga, published author of the Book *"Pointing Children To Christ- 52 weeks Family Devotional"*- held my hand, walked with me, and prayed with me in developing the raw work into a book! As my partner in this journey, Lilian took the raw materials of each section and chapter and met me where I was by thoroughly reviewing my manuscript. She is such a great encourager who makes you feel you are already an accomplished author. I would not hesitate to recommend Lilian as an editor to any emerging Christian author via familyrebuilders@gmail.com.

Lydia Chola Waiyaki, whom I met on October 21, 2022, so greatly encouraged, and positively impacted me by telling me her own experience of how she went through the journey of writing a real-life story about her son and nephew in her book, *A Journey with Christ*, which encouraged me to complete my manuscript and have this book published through WestBow Press.

CHAPTER 1

A HISTORICAL BACKGROUND

Upon my father's demise, some people came by to visit our mother. In their conversation, they asked her what she had planned for her daughters now that the vision bearer and the household provider was no more.

Without batting an eyelid, our mother, full of faith, responded, "Yes, I may be widowed, alone, yet I am not alone. Yes, their earthly father is gone, but the great Jehovah Jireh is our real provider, and He is more than enough. He is alive forever more and will be there to take very good care of us."

She was certain that our earthly father's dream for his daughters would come to pass. Our mother faithfully prayed this dream through, and we are witnesses who have lived to behold it with our very own eyes. Hers is a narrative of faith coming alive, one that continues to influence us long after her departure from this world.

Years later, the two daughters she faced the lion with found themselves studying abroad, one in the United Kingdom and the other in the United States of America. There were significant moments, such as when these two daughters met across the Atlantic

Ocean for higher education studies and when they converged with delegates in the central part of Africa as key players in influencing decisions on a global United Nations platform. There are days when all her four surviving daughters still gather to worship the Lord together, rejoicing in Yahweh for the joy of being destined for heaven, where we shall meet our mother again. Our mother lived to see her grandchildren and great-grandchildren before she went to be with the Lord at ninety-two years.

The emphasis of this book is on an intentional mother, grandmother, and great-grandmother who left a spiritual legacy for those who came after her. Through her, we have learned to honor and worship the true God; Jehovah is His name. Our mother left us an inheritance with eternal value, a treasure far more important than the world's temporal inheritance of money and property. We, her children, received an imperishable, godly heritage from her that we long to pass on, just as it was passed down to us. She left us a legacy of faith in Christ that guarantees a full inheritance kept in heaven forever if we remain true to Jehovah. Our mother taught us to depend on God as our dependable Father. One of her most favorite songs was "With Ties of Love," based on a key scripture in the book of Hosea, "I led Israel along with my ropes of kindness and love. I lifted the yoke from his neck, and I myself stooped to feed him" (Hosea 11:4 NLT).

Our mother would often remind us of the God who neither forgets nor forsakes His children, just like she had made up her mind to never abandon her own children. Following my earthly father's demise, she daily accentuated that we had a heavenly Father who cared much more than she or our dad ever could. She pointed us to His Word in the book of Isaiah, "Never! Can a mother forget her nursing child? Can she feel no love for the child she has borne? But even if that were possible, I would not forget you!" (Isaiah 49:15 NLT).

Thinking about her legacy of faith, I am forever grateful that our mother left for us what is acclaimed in Proverbs 13:22a, "an inheritance for her children's children."

My Mother's Footprints

Everyone leaves a legacy. We all leave footprints behind us. Every one of us will be remembered for something, whether good, bad, or indifferent. Those who mourn our departure from this world will talk about the ways we interacted with them and tell of how we either influenced or neglected their lives. While some people leave assets, property, or money for those behind them, some leave a legacy of faith, an invisible but far more valuable treasure loaded with eternal benefits.

In telling our mother's story, we believe it is important to leave a Christlike legacy for one's future generations, a set of footprints that will outlast one's lifetime. We also believe that we cannot do this on our own. However, we can do it through sharing the gospel of Jesus Christ with others, as the gospel brings life. We therefore need to share with others the need to receive Christ's free offer of mercy and to allow Jesus to fill us with the Holy Spirit. Then we become witnesses as He empowers and teaches us to love Him and others and influence our families, community, people, nation, continent, and world.

This is what the Paris Evangelical Missionary Society (PEMS) at Nasikena village in Sefula, founded by the missionary François Coillard, the Basotho Missionaries, and others did for our great-grandparents, our grandparents, our parents, our mother, us, and our children. We are committed to passing on this legacy of faith, as we are witness to the far-reaching outcomes transcending generations. "One generation will commend Your works to the next, and will proclaim Your mighty acts" (Psalm 145:4).

Our Lineage: A Christian Heritage

We wish to recognize and honor our late mother as a remarkable woman whose most striking quality was intentionality. She was deliberate about building us a legacy of faith and instilling Christian values in us, a heritage we continue to be grateful for. We give thanks to the Lord Jehovah for the seed planted by an obedient servant of God, François Coillard, and his wife, Christina Mackintosh, daughter of a Scottish Baptist minister and a psalmist who played songs on the harmonica. They diligently worked alongside the Basotho evangelists in Nasikena village in Sefula over a century ago.

Whereas Reverend François Coillard was a renowned evangelist, his wife, who hailed from a Baptist background, was very well-versed in scriptures. She was instrumental in grounding the women from Sefula with the Word of God, which she taught them systematically.

Receiving Missionaries in Sefula

Reverend François Coillard arrived in Sefula in 1884 and officially established the church with the Litunga's agreement, the Lozi King Lewanika, in 1886. Our great-grandparents received the man of God, accepted Christ as their personal Savior and Lord, and passed on this heritage to their children, who in turn passed it on to their children and to their children's children to the glory of God. Our prayer for the next generation is that this faith legacy continues as we believe and pray the written Word in Paul's letter to Timothy. This shall be so because we believe in the power of the Holy Spirit; if we ask in faith, we believe the Lord will hear and empower us to continue praying and passing on the spiritual legacy we have received from our mother, grandmother, and great-grandparents to our children, just as Timothy received from his mother and grandmother in 2 Timothy 1:2–7 (NLT).

> Timothy, I thank God for you—the God I serve with a clear conscience, just as my ancestors did. Night and day I constantly remember you in my prayers. I long to see you again, for I remember your tears as we parted. And I will be filled with joy when we are together again. I remember your genuine faith, for

you share the faith that first filled your grandmother Lois and your mother, Eunice. And I know that same faith continues strong in you. This is why I remind you to fan into flames the spiritual gift God gave you when I laid my hands on you. For God has not given us a spirit of fear and timidity, but of power, love, and self-discipline.

Generational Blessings

Led by the Holy Spirit, Muluti (Muruti) Reverend François Coillard arrived in Sefula at Nasikena, where three brothers, Bo Ndate Monde, Bo Ndate Sikatana, and Bo Ndate Ndambila, received him. Bo Ndate Monde was our great-grandfather, father to our maternal grandmother, Bo Wamusheke Lisulo (Bo Ma-Wabei). Along with being mother to our mother, Bo Wabei Lisulo (Bo Ma-Matauka), she was mother to Mwangala (Bo Ma-Victor); Daniel Muchiwa Lisulo, the first Zambian state counsel (SC); Muteletwa (Bo Ma-Mukatimui); and Mwangala (Bo Ma-Lisulo).

My maternal uncle, Mr. Daniel Lisulo, became the legal counsel for Zambia African National Congress (ZANC) during the struggle for Zambia's independence and represented the United National Independence Party (UNIP) after ZANC was banned. He established the external wing of UNIP and set up the UNIP operations base in Dar es Salaam, Tanzania. During the late Dr. Kenneth Kaunda's government, Mr. Daniel Lisulo, SC, held various positions, including Solicitor General (SG) and Attorney General (AG). Besides serving as the very first Zambian SC, he went on to become the prime minister and head of government from 1978 through 1981.

The fourth-born, Bo Muteletwa (Bo Ma-Mukatimui), was a nurse and later took on administrative roles following further training. The fifth and last born, Bo Mwangala (Bo Ma-Lisulo), was among the second cohort of African registered nurses trained in Mpilo,

Bulawayo, Southern Rhodesia, now known as Zimbabwe. She held several senior positions, including sister in charge, matron, and chief nursing officer, among others, at various hospitals in Zambia, including Lewanika General Hospital, Ndola Central Hospital, and the University Teaching Hospital (UTH).

The second brother to Bo Ndate Monde, our great-grandfather, was Bo Ndate Sikatana, the grandfather to Hon. Mundia Sikatana, the honorable minister of agriculture in the Mwanawasa government. He was the government minister who introduced the growing of winter maize in Zambia and stood against the pressure and insistence by donors to provide Zambia with GMO maize seeds. He demonstrated integrity in his assignment as a cabinet minister and received accolades from not only Zambia but from the African continent as a man of integrity. By introducing the growing of winter maize in Zambia, Mr. Mundia Sikatana ensured that Zambia could harvest her staple food twice a year, making her self-sufficient in food for the first time in her history.

Mr. and Mrs. Sikatana.

Bo Ndate Sikatana was also the grandfather to Mr. Mwanang'ono Kufekisa Mbikusita-Lewanika, the firstborn son of Litunga (King) Mbikusita Lewanika 11. He was among the first one hundred graduates at Zambia's independence and in the first cohort of Zambians to obtain a bachelor's degree in education. He received his training from both South Africa and America, served among the first black African teachers at Munali National School for Boys, and was the first Zambian principal of Chizongwe and Lundazi Secondary Schools in the Eastern Province of Zambia.

The third brother to Bo Ndate Monde, who was also there to receive the first missionary, was Bo Ndate Ndambila. He was grandfather to Mr. Imasiku Saasa of Shimabale farms, popularly known as Liwanguwangu during the then-Zambia Broadcasting Services (ZBS) programs before it rebranded to Zambia National Broadcasting Corporation (ZNBC). He was one of the first managers at the Zambia National Insurance Corporation (ZNIC).

This is how François Coillard was received in Nasikena village in Sefula, as narrated to us by Nasikena elders, our great-grandparents, and grandparents and confirmed by our grandmother and later our own mother.

A Church Is Birthed

François Coillard arrived at Nasikena village in Sefula in 1884 from Socha, hungry, tired, thirsty, and longing for some water to drink. At Nasikena, there was a running stream where the villagers would often be found washing clothes from or sourcing water for other cleaning purposes. However, the Nasikena people did not use the stream water for drinking; instead, they had a protected spring well from where they drew fresh and clean drinking water. By the protected spring well, they had placed several containers to help preserve the purity of the water. One was specifically for drawing water directly from the well; the other was for pouring out the water into other containers they took home for drinking. They also had designated water containers for cooking, drinking, and washing. The vessel used to draw out water from the protected spring well was carefully preserved and positioned at a special place above the ground, *Kalani*, to avoid water contamination.

On arrival at the protected spring well at Nasikena village, François Coillard requested drinking water and was granted permission to draw some. He took the specialized vessel from the Kalani, the elevated place, and drew the water. Then he went ahead to drink deeply, directly drinking from the same container, an unacceptable practice in the village. After he drank, the Nasikena village people discarded the container and explained that it could not be used for drawing water anymore since it was contaminated by being used for another purpose.

From this incident, François Coillard named this village Nasikena, meaning the source and mother of a very clean place and hygienic people. François Coillard also knelt and prayed, and the Holy Spirit confirmed to him that this was the place where he was to set up the first Paris station named Evangelical Missionary Society (PEMS) in Bulozi.

Founded in 1822, PEMS (Société des Missions Evangéliques de Paris), Mission de Paris united local mission support groups in parts of Europe such as France, Switzerland, and Italy in collaboration with churches such as the Lutheran, Reformed, Baptists, and Methodists until its dissolution in 1971. In 1829, its very first missionaries were dispatched to South Africa, since at that time Protestants were forbidden access to French colonial territories.[1]

François Coillard set up camp on the outskirts of Nasikena village. The three brothers—Bo Ndate Monde (Bo Joana/John, also known as Abraham), Bo Ndate Sikatana (Bo Zakeya/Zacchaeus), and Bo Ndate Ndambila (Bo Petrosi/Peter)—were observing keenly and came forward to help guard his safety. They were aware of the wild animals like lions, tigers, and leopards that roamed the area,

---

[1] https://referenceworks.brillonline.com/entries/religion-past-and-present/paris-evangelical-missionary-society-SIM_024366)

particularly at night, and cared enough to help François Coillard erect his tent by their Nasikena village for his physical protection.

The place where François Coillard erected his first tent was called Sefula because it was a lush grazing area where the streams of fresh waters flowed from Sefula Musindi, meaning a spring/well of water, and where both plants and animals flourished. The second meaning for Sefula was based on the language spoken by François Coillard and his team from Paris, France. They spoke the French language, which was translated as Sefula (Sifula) in the local Silozi/Sikololo language.

At the place where François Coillard pitched camp, a beacon made of nails was established, marking the significant missionary arrival and presence at Sefula in Bulozi. This signified the founding of the first-ever Paris Evangelical Missionary Society (PEMS) church in Bulozi in 1884. This church thrived and became host to a transformational center that included a school, a vocational/trades/skills training center, and later a teacher training school in 1886. François Coillard, full of the Holy Spirit, was led to reach his first converts and students: the three brothers (Bo Ndate Monde, Bo Ndate Sikatana, and Bo Ndate Ndambila), their spouses, and other family members from Nasikena village in Sefula.

Interestingly, the conversation between François Coillard, who spoke Sesotho, and the three brothers, who spoke Silozi/Sikololo, was effective, and they could therefore communicate. The three brothers informed François Coillard that they had a Litunga (king). At the time of François Coillard's arrival in Sefula, there was a power struggle for the Litungaship at the king's palace in Lealui. Eventually though, King Lewanika established himself as ruler and became the Litunga who granted approval for the official establishment of the PEMS in the Bulozi region.

The Litunga's (King's) Conversion to Christianity

The three brothers advised on the importance of meeting with the king. They offered to arrange for François Coillard to meet with the Litunga (king) in Lealui, which was and still remains the Litunga's capital during the dry season, whereas Limulunga, on higher ground, is the capital during the flood period. The meeting was successful, as King Lewanika welcomed the man of God, converted to Christianity, sent his sons to study at Sefula, and allowed François Coillard to set up another mission station at Lwatile, adjacent to the Lealui palace. This mission station was called Lwatile because François Coillard and the Basotho evangelists took time to give thanks to God there for His favor and the increase they had witnessed so far.

The Litunga's warm reception and conversion contributed to the immense growth of the number of believers as the Lord continued to establish His kingdom in the area. François Coillard had a common practice wherever he established a mission station. He would pray aloud and declare the goodness of God and his unwavering trust and belief in Christ Jesus. He would quote the Bible passage in Romans 1:16–17 (NLT), "For I am not ashamed of this Good News about Christ. It is the power of God at work, saving everyone who believes—the Jew first and also the Gentile."

This good news teaches us how God makes us right in His sight by grace, through faith in Jesus Christ. "It is through faith that a righteous person has life." This is how the place earned its name Lwatile where the just would live by faith.

Collage of photos relating to François Coillard.

Français Coillard was a French-born, Protestant missionary and explorer who served diligently in Central Africa. He joined the PEMS School of Missions under Eugène Casalis, together with Adolphe Mabille. Upon his ordination in 1857, he set sail to Lesotho with the second generation of PEMS missionaries. In partnership with a team of Basotho evangelists from Leribe in Lesotho, they established the Sefula mission. He was married to Christina Mackintosh (1829–1891), a daughter of a Scottish Baptist minister, whom he had met in Paris in 1861. Coillard was dispatched to Leribe, a town that had been placed under the authority of Molapo, a son of Moshoeshoe, which became his home for twenty years. He spoke excellent Sesotho; wrote hymns, poems, and stories; and served as a translator for content that was applied in the schools.

Barotseland was a country experiencing political upheaval and turmoil in 1884 with King Lewanika exiled. During one of his missionary expeditions, Coillard managed to establish friendly, diplomatic relations with Lewanika, who was soon back in power. In March 1886, he was received by Lewanika at Lealui, the kingdom's capital. He actively coordinated missionary excursions with Basotho evangelists and planted new churches in the Kingdom. He founded the Zambezi mission in 1885 and was received by Lewanika, king of the Barotse, first at Sefula and later at Lealui, Zambia. He also was instrumental in establishing a strong network of Zambezians in Europe alongside Alfred Bertrand for mission support. Coillard died at Lealui in 1904, and both he and his wife were buried at Sefula, leaving a rich, godly legacy (Marc R. Spindler 2007).

Besides the legacy of faith through evangelizing through Barotseland, many more mission stations were birthed, including among others Lwatile, Lukona, Mabumbu, Limulunga, Mukoko, Mwandi, Sesheke, Nalolo, and Senanga. There was also a major impact on the development of education in Barotseland and Zambia. The first school set up at Sefula on March 4, 1887, had twenty pupils, who included future rulers like Litia Lewanika (Litunga Yeta III) and Mukamba (future Ngambela). The class of 1887 also included the three brothers (Bo Ndate Monde, Bo Ndate Sikatana, and Bo Ndate Ndambila), our great-grandparents from Nasikena village who had received and helped François Coillard pitch his tent at Sefula in 1884. Sefula mission was established as a transformational center inclusive of the church, the academic part of the school; the trade school offering carpentry, woodwork, and metalwork; a health center; a women's development and crafts center; and a school for the visually impaired.

PEMS Sefula school class of 1887.

The people of Sefula were among the first literate people in Barotseland. The Sefula mission produced leaders who later took on leadership roles on the political scene, including forming part of the initial cabinet ministers during the reign of Kenneth Kaunda, the very first post-independence government in Zambia.

The whole Nasikena village was united in purpose, as Jesus prayed in John 17:22–26 (NLT).

> I have given them the glory you gave me, so they may be one as we are one. I am in them and you are in me. May they experience such perfect unity that the world will know that you sent me and that you love them as much as you love me. Father, I want these whom you have given me to be with me where I am. Then they can see all the glory you gave me because you loved me even before the world began! "O righteous Father, the world doesn't know you, but I do; and these disciples know you sent me. I have revealed you to them, and I will continue to do so.

Then your love for me will be in them, and I will be in them. "May they be brought to complete unity to let the world know that you sent me and have loved them even as you have loved me."

The Nasikena village community believed that God called each one of them individually and corporately to represent Christ to the world. Their authentic faith ensured that their faith and walk in Christ unified them in the purposes of Christ.

A Village Is Transformed

Just as it happened in the early church in the biblical book of Acts, the villagers of Nasikena lived it out. Unsurprisingly, the entire village came to the saving knowledge of Jesus Christ during the times when our great-grandparents, grandparents, and parents lived.

> Then the whole population of Lydda and Sharon saw Aeneas walking around, and they turned to the Lord. There was a believer in Joppa named Tabitha (which in Greek is Dorcas). She was always doing kind things for others and helping the poor. About this time, she became ill and died. Her body was washed for burial and laid in an upstairs room. But the believers had heard that Peter was nearby at Lydda, so they sent two men to beg him, "Please come as soon as possible!" So, Peter returned with them; and as soon as he arrived, they took him to the upstairs room. The room was filled with widows who were weeping and showing him the coats and other clothes Dorcas had made for them. But Peter asked them all to leave the room; then he knelt and prayed. Turning to the body he said, "Get up, Tabitha." And she opened her eyes! When she saw

> Peter, she sat up! He gave her his hand and helped
> her up. Then he called in the widows and all the
> believers, and he presented her to them alive. The
> news spread through the whole town, and many
> believed in the Lord. And Peter stayed a long time
> in Joppa, living with Simon, a tanner of hides. (Acts
> 9:35–42 NLT)

It happened before in Lydda, Sharon, and Joppa in biblical times, regions being won to the Lord. The same Holy Spirit was moving to see to it that a passionate investment of faith in Jesus Christ transformed the whole village of Nasikena in Sefula. People engaged in diligent devotion and preaching the Word, passionate prayer with a deep yearning for the Holy Spirit. There was genuine conversion, humility, unity, and a hunger for the knowledge of God's Word and His ways. Studying the Word of God and engaging in prayer became a lifestyle for the villagers.

Our great-uncles, Bo Simushi and Bo Sikambo, often told us the stories and shared the testimonies of how the villagers prayed early in the morning before sunrise, before going to the fields or work and before the children went to school. They held evening devotionals where they spent the time around the fireplace, sharing and dividing the Word of God, just like the people of Berea did in Acts 7:11–12 (NLT).

> And the people of Berea were more open-minded
> than those in Thessalonica, and they listened eagerly
> to Paul's message. They searched the Scriptures Day
> after day to see if Paul and Silas were teaching the
> truth. As a result, many Jews believed, as did many
> of the prominent Greek women and men.

In the beginning, most of the people were either illiterate or semi-literate in the written language; therefore, of the few who could, they read the scriptures out loud for everyone else. They had fun with

Bible quizzes, sung the scripture verses, and told Bible stories as they worked. This seeking of God's kingdom first caused Him to add all other things to these dedicated villagers, changing the spiritual and physical atmosphere of the whole village of Nasikena. As I think about it now, God's Word still stands for your family, your city, your nation, and your own life today. "But seek first the kingdom of God and His righteousness, and all these things will be added unto you" (Matthew 6:33).

Humility, Compassion, and Love for People

Nasikena villagers served God with humility in their everyday work. They did not work for recognition by men, but instead they did everything as unto the Lord and gave all the glory to God. The villagers were known for their kindness, love for all people, compassion, and humility because they were being ruled by and used of God. One woman from another part of Barotseland who got married into Nasikena village, specifically into the Sikatana family, Mrs. Monde Milupi Sikatana shared her story of how amazed she was at the warm manner she was received as a daughter-in-law. She was given the same privileges as the daughters born in Nasikena village and swore to carry on the same love culture into the generations after her. This then confirms the scripture as written in Psalms 25:9–10 (NLT), "He leads the humble in doing right, teaching them his way. The Lord leads with unfailing love and faithfulness all who keep his covenant and obey his demands."

Mrs. Monde Sikatana.

Unity of Purpose by the Nasikena Family

In Nasikena village, no member of the family went without food or shelter above their head. As long as one of them had something, they all had something. The physically strong people helped to construct houses for those who were less able. They shared food in common. The widows among them were taken very good care of and allowed to cultivate their late husband's fields. The very poor were adopted into the village as part of the family. Every visitor who passed by Nasikena village was received and fed like any other family member. They worked together in cooking, harvesting, and caring for the less privileged, including those with disabilities. In a similar way, they adopted and daily lived out the early church practice where

All the believers were one in heart and mind. No one claimed that any of their possessions was their own, but they shared everything they had. With great power the apostles continued to testify to the resurrection of the Lord Jesus. And God's grace was so powerfully at work in them all that there were no needy persons among them. For from time to time those who owned land or houses sold them, brought the money from the sales and put it at the apostles' feet, and it was distributed to anyone who had need. (Acts 4:32–34)

A Miracle in the Nasikena Village: The Case of Evangelists, Bo Sikambo and Bo Simushi

The blind see; the lame walk. Two of our great-uncles, Bo Sikambo and Bo Simushi, were physically and visually challenged, respectively. Owing to their disabilities, they could neither go to the fields to work nor attend school when their peers registered for formal schooling. From the truth discovered during regular Bible study, the villagers in Nasikena decided to apply those truths, continually prayed for the healing of these young men, and consistently provided for these two young men. Daily, the villagers would pray for their healing and then leave them behind while they went to work the fields. They ensured there were sufficient drinks, food, and comfortable shelter until their return from the day's work or occupations.

There was no instant miraculous healing, but the Nasikena-Sefula people earnestly continued in prayer over these two. They prayed for their healing, claiming the books of Acts (Likezo), trusting in God through the power of the Holy Spirit and appropriating what is written in Acts 1:8 (NLT), "But you will receive power when the Holy Spirit comes upon you. And you will be my witnesses, telling people about me everywhere—in Jerusalem, throughout Judea, in Samaria, and to the ends of the earth."

They evangelized through conducting rallies (Sikundi) and went about as fishers of men. Rooted in the Word, they prayed for the sick and expected the signs to follow them because they believed, as instructed in the Great Commission and as promised in Mark 16:15–20 (NLT).

> And then he told them, "Go into all the world and preach the Good News to everyone. Anyone who believes and is baptized will be saved. But anyone who refuses to believe will be condemned. These miraculous signs will accompany those who believe: They will cast out demons in my name, and they will speak in new languages. They will be able to handle snakes with safety, and if they drink anything poisonous, it won't hurt them. They will be able to place their hands on the sick, and they will be healed." When the Lord Jesus had finished talking with them, he was taken up into heaven and sat down in the place of honor at God's right hand. And the disciples went everywhere and preached, and the Lord worked through them, confirming what they said by many miraculous signs.

Now, the story about these young men is told to date. We heard it from our mother, our grandmother, and other people from Nasikena. They tell of how one fateful morning, as was the normal practice, the men, women, and children of Nasikena/Sefula prayed as usual before departing to their engagements around and beyond the village. As was the norm, the two boys with disabilities were left in the village, having had their basic needs taken care of to await the return of the rest later in the day.

It was an astounding sight when the villagers returned that day! Around midday, the people who came home found the two boys whole! *Bo Sikambo was walking; he had never walked before! And Bo Simushi could see! He had been as blind as blind can get! It was nothing short of a miracle!*

People were astonishingly glad. It was just like what they had read in the book of Acts when believers were interceding for Peter in Acts (Likezo) 12:1–11 and he had a miraculous escape from prison. Likewise, the Sefula villagers had been praying for the two boys with disabilities. They had just witnessed a miracle but were still pleasantly surprised. Their first reaction was to wonder in disbelief and sheer amazement at what the Lord had done in their midst. However, they later came to the realization that God had answered their prayers, and oh, what a joyful song of worship and praise to the Most High God resounded from their homes! "the blind see, the lame walk, those with leprosy are cured, the deaf hear, the dead are raised to life, and the Good News is being preached to the poor" (Matthew 11:5).

Dear reader, you must be wondering whatever became of those two young men. Both Bo Simushi and Bo Sikambo became evangelists. I personally met Bo Sikambo, who mostly carried a coat and three books: the Holy Bible, the Silozi Redemption hymn book, and the Munembo (praise song book). He traversed the breadth and length of Bulozi-Barotseland sharing the gospel of Jesus Christ and anchored his ministry on Luke 9:1–6 (NLT).

> One day Jesus called together his twelve disciples and gave them power and authority to cast out all demons and to heal all diseases. Then he sent them out to tell everyone about the Kingdom of God and to heal the sick. "Take nothing for your journey," he instructed them. "Don't take a walking stick, a traveler's bag, food, money, or even a change of clothes. Wherever you go, stay in the same house until you leave town. And if a town refuses to welcome you, shake its dust from your feet as you leave to show that you have abandoned those people to their fate." So, they began their circuit of the villages, preaching the Good News and healing the sick.

Bo Sikambo was sold out as a disciple of Jesus, a living testimony of what the Lord can do. He was miraculously healed of polio. He was once lame, but as soon as he miraculously walked, he decided to walk for Jesus for the rest of his life on earth. In simple faith, he took the Word and literary applied it to himself, his ministry, and the people he faithfully ministered to in Barotseland. He never lacked; he would testify that there was no day he ever went without food. He always had food on his table and always had somewhere to sleep as he navigated Barotseland as an evangelist. When his coat and clothes became dirty or aged, someone would be at hand to help wash, iron, or replace them with a new set of clothing! Jehovah Jireh cared for him. "But my God shall supply all your need according to his riches in glory by Christ Jesus" (Philippians 4:19).

CHAPTER 2

BO MA-MATAUKA: THE CHURCH PLANTER

A Testimony by Firstborn Daughter, Bo Matauka

According to her firstborn daughter, Bo Matauka, one outstanding aspect of our mother's faith was that she never missed a fellowship but consistently conducted Bible study with family, relatives, and other fellow Christians. Family attendance to Sunday church services week after week was modeled by our mother. If she happened to be absent due to an inevitable circumstance, the congregants would be quick to notice it and immediately inquire about her whereabouts because her ministry would be greatly missed.

Bo Matauka, firstborn daughter of Bo Ma-Matauka.

Our mother ensured there were regular visits to the needy in her community as well as mid-weekday fellowship meetings wherever she lived. Such were her non-negotiables. "Pure and undefiled religion before our God and Father is this: to care for orphans and widows in their distress, and to keep oneself from being polluted by the world" (James 1:27).

Bo Ma-Matauka would never miss the early-morning prayer meetings held at the school, wherever she could be teaching. A missionary, Ms. A. Jalla, identified the gifting her in her voice and instituted her as a psalmist and evangelist. Mum would often be heard praising, worshipping, and singing her way into the day early in the morning.

Having grown up in Sefula, she was accustomed to personal devotion as a way of life. Sunday was a Sabbath day to be kept holy according to God's command. Prayer time was not an option; neither was time for Bible study and Bible quizzes. She diligently followed this culture and established it as a family tradition. She taught us to seek the Lord and love Him with all our heart, mind, might, and soul. "And thou shalt love the Lord thy God with all thy heart, and with all thy soul, and with all thy mind, and with all thy strength: this is the first commandment" (Mark 12:30).

At Mukwamalundu on the Barotse Plains, she would join her parents in canoes, navigating the choppy waters to attend fellowship and church services. They would cross canals to get to Mukoko, even during the flood season. The floods did not deter her from attending church and meeting with fellow believers. As a married woman residing in either Lusaka, Chilenje, or Matero, she would prioritize finding a church or a Christian fellowship group she could plug into and serve soon after relocating.

Upon her husband's demise, she chose to specifically teach in Christian mission schools, where she could fellowship with other brethren and manage to attend church services regularly. Bo Ma-Matauka put God first all her days and taught others to do so. "But seek ye first the kingdom of God, and his righteousness; and all these things shall be added unto you" (Matthew 6:33).

Planting the Church

In the late 1990s, she called her family, her children and siblings, to express the desire and decision to obey God's instruction. She admitted that for a while, she had felt strongly that the Lord was calling her to plant a community church on her father's land. She made a passionate plea for everyone present to contribute toward building the foundation of this community church.

She was very clear on the instructions God had given her, to model the church design according to that of Sefula PEMS Transformational Center. When the family inquired about the specific denomination she would operate under, she responded that God simply wanted a church established. She firmly stood on the truth that when we get to heaven, it is what we do with the Great Commission that will win the day, not the denominations that people ascribe to. Rather, the ultimate decision would be whether we accepted or rejected Jesus Christ as our personal Savior and Lord. And just like that, Bo Ma-Matauka planted the Malengwa family church, which is now called Malengwa UCZ Congregation, in obedience to the prompting of the Holy Spirit.

Mukwamalundu community UCZ church, Malengwa Congregation.

Some of the people who supported the foundation.

The late Rev. Mulowa, who went to be with the Lord in 2022, authorized the construction of the church by Mum at Malengwa on the land that her parental uncle, Chief Libumbu-Mutakela-Alibandila, gave her. The other members of the UCZ Western Presbytery initially resisted the idea, thinking that as the vision was to have a church on the Sefula transformation model, this would be a breakaway church. Through family contributions, however, my mother was determined and sought the support of her family to realize the vision to plant a church, notwithstanding the opposition. The foundation started with seed money from several people who believed in this noble cause:

- Her late brother, Mr. Daniel Muchiwa Lisulo, former prime minister in the Republic of Zambia
- Her late young sister, Muteletwa, Mrs. Mwanalushi
- Her second-born daughter, Wamusheke Njebele
- Her third-born daughter, Rose Kashembe Sakala
- Her fourth-born daughter, Sibeso Mukoboto Luswata, author of this book
- Reverend Ms. Kalubi Muyunda
- Mr. Likukela (Miyanda-Namakau's grandfather)
- Mr. Konga Ikasaya
- Mr. and Mrs. Koota
- Mr. and Mrs. Mutumba

Soon after, the local community members came together and established a fundraising team, *Musali Yema uyahe Keleke; Muna Yema uyahe Keleke*, based on a positive competitive fundraising model. This helped to accelerate the construction works as each group worked hard to be the best among the groups instead of basing it on individual-based competition.

Today, UCZ Malengwa Congregation stands strong and continues to impact the local community. The congregants included members from Mongu Teachers' college and the nearby schools; therefore, it was quickly approved with Reverend Uwafwa Revious Chisha being assigned as the very first clergy. Led by my mother, the Malengwa UCZ congregation took complete charge over the clergy needs, eventually sending him to train as a fully fledged reverend. He graduated as a reverend in 2016.

After his graduation, the Western Presbytery assigned him to Lilelelo in Mongu, and after that, he was transferred to Livingstone in Southern Province. This small church planted by our mother was soon providing ministers to the UCZ Western Presbytery. In August 2017, more than three thousand people were hosted there with an overflow hosted at Mongu Teachers' College for a presbytery event, as there was no more room.

Many years later, Bo Ma-Matauka's send-off service was held on the same church grounds on Wednesday, February 21, 2018. It was conducted by ministers from different denominations, confirming indeed that she was a kingdom person! She had unified many through practicing Christlike love for brethren.

The Malengwa UCZ congregation continues to grow, and at the time of writing her story, the church she planted has established five satellite congregations at Lilundu, Miulwe, Mweeke, Mawawa, and Nangula. These satellite centers are used for evangelism and ongoing support for discipleship classes. The Malengwa UCZ church elders regularly visit these satellites to provide both spiritual and material support. They take turns leading and administering the Holy Communion.

CHAPTER 3

A RICH LEGACY BY BO WABEI LISULO, A.K.A. BO MA-MATAUKA

Our Mother's Legacy: Our Heritage

Our mother was the granddaughter to the eldest of the three brothers who received François Coillard at Nasikena village in 1884. Her grandfather, Bo Ndate Monde, Muyambango, was baptized as Johana (John) and commonly known to his peers as Abraham. His brother, Bo Ndate Sikatana, Munalula, was baptized as Zakeya (Zacchaeus). Zakeya fathered Eleazor Sikatana, one of the first jeans teachers in Bulozi. The third brother was Bo Ndate Ndambila, baptized as Petrosi (Peter).

Our mother, Bo Ma-Matauka, believed in Jesus Christ as her personal Savior and Lord. She shared the Word of God whenever and wherever any opportunity presented itself and left a lasting spiritual legacy according to the instruction in the Word of God, which she abided by as her light and lamp.

O my people, listen to my instructions. Open your ears to what I am saying, for I will speak to you in a parable. I will teach you hidden lessons from our past stories we have heard and known, stories our ancestors handed down to us. We will not hide these truths from our children; we will tell the next generation about the glorious deeds of the Lord, about His power and His mighty wonders. For He issued His laws to Jacob; He gave His instructions to Israel. He commanded our ancestors to teach them to their children, so the next generation might know them—even the children not yet born—and they in turn will teach their own children. So, each generation should set its hope anew on God, not forgetting his glorious miracles and obeying his commands. (Psalm 78:1–7 NLT)

A Legacy of Faith/Thumelo

Mum believed that God existed to be worshipped, that there is heaven and hell, and that God rewards those who earnestly seek Him. By faith, she accepted Jesus Christ as her personal Savior and Lord. By faith, she believed God in what He had revealed to her regarding her daughters. Our mother still lived by faith in her last two and half years on earth, even on her sickbed before going to be with her Lord. She was never ashamed of stating categorically what she believed and whom she believed in and that Jehovah, Yahweh, was her God. All this confirms the Word, which she so cherished in Hebrews 11:6 (NLT), "And it is impossible to please God without faith. Anyone who wants to come to him must believe that God exists and that he rewards those who sincerely seek him."

A Legacy of Hope/Tsepo/Sepo

Our mother always declared that her hope was established on the blood poured out on the cross at Calvary and in the forgiveness of her sins because the Lord Jesus died for her on the cross. She had unwavering hope in her maker, that if we believe in the Lord Jesus Christ as our personal Savior and Lord, and because He died for our sins on the cross at Calvary, we shall have eternal life and be with Him through eternity. She often quoted Romans 8:25 (NLT), "But if we look forward to something we don't yet have, we must wait patiently and confidently." Our mother persevered and never tired of worshipping and serving the Lord.

A Legacy of Love/Lerato/Lilato

Bo Ma-Matauka was a woman who loved greatly and did not discriminate against the disadvantaged in her community. She embraced all those who came into her space. As a teacher, she accommodated and accepted so many schoolchildren who had nowhere to stay and some who came from very faraway places where there were no schools. She physically accommodated many of them in her own house. She was a compassionate woman of influence who impacted so many lives. While she lived, during her illness as well as at her funeral, throngs of people testified about the love of God that flowed through her, impacting either them or their many children. When taking her body remains for burial from Lusaka to Mongu and as we approached Mongu, scores and scores of people stopped the hearse with us to pay their last respects, and some of them just wanted to escort her remains for the last five kilometers to her home, all because of what she had done either for them, their children, or their grandchildren and the church in Bulozi.

The different church denominations in Bulozi paid their respects and sang of her accolades. The clergy recommended to have her buried among the heroes of faith either at Sefula or Mabumbu missions. However, this was not to be as she had willed that she be buried and gathered with her parents at Mukwamalundu village, Malengwa, Mongu district. When we got to her home village, we still found scores of people waiting to pay their last respects. At the church she planted, many people were also waiting to pay their last respects. Our mother understood love and compassion as true influences that go beyond affluence.

A Legacy of Obedience/Tundamo

Bo Ma-Matauka valued obedience to God's calling and daily walking in His ways. She would often remind us that there was no way she could have attained what she did except with His help, His power, and His faithfulness. God had endowed her with multiple spiritual gifts, and her response to His calling was to serve, love, obey, and worship Him wholeheartedly. Our mother was a faithful steward over what she was entrusted with and diligently obeyed the Word of God.

As she lived her life before us, she modeled obedience and proclaimed God's faithfulness in fulfilling His promises to her and us. The dreams she and her late husband, our dad, held close to heart about their children and the words they spoke over our lives years before were fulfilled by her God through her sustained prayers. This reminded us of how faithful God was at keeping His promises, just as He fulfilled the promises to Abraham, Joseph, and David. He still did it in our generation, fulfilling the promises through our mother to us, despite us losing our father at an early age.

A Legacy to Treasure God's Word/Linzwi

Our mother loved and trusted in God, meditated on the Word of God, and acted on it. She organized and conducted morning and evening devotionals in the home with all her children, relatives, and any guests who visited during the designated fellowship time. She dwelt in His presence daily, meaning the Trinity resided in her home, and we experienced Him and His manifest presence and goodness, just like Jesus promised in John 14:23–24 (NLT), "Jesus replied, 'All who love me will do what I say. My Father will love them, and we will come and make our home with each of them. Anyone who doesn't love me will not obey me. And remember, my words are not my own. What I am telling you is from the Father who sent me.'"

Bo Ma-Matauka always had her Bible near and studied it often. She embraced the Word of God, appropriated it in her everyday life, and established a deep personal relationship with God. She got to know Him more and more, understand His ways, and perceive His leading. In the church she planted, she ensured they engaged in weekly Bible study quizzes that encouraged all members to study the Word daily.

Growing up, we all had to be ready to share the Word during home devotionals. Bo Ma-Matauka had a typical approach of randomly picking anyone in the circle to lead the evening Bible study. This put every child on our toes to let the Word dwell richly in us and to be ready with the Word in and out of season. We sang scriptural songs, created the spoken word from what we were studying with her, and even formed a family choir. This musical group was always prepared to sing any time during evangelism sessions or at church whenever we would be required to. We learned to evangelize without cowering, sharing the Word of God from an early age as Mum expected us to do so during Sikundi (fishing of men rallies) as well as at Butoya camps. These were her simple open secrets to raising a godly offspring and establishing faith in her generation.

CHAPTER 4

MEET BO WABEI LISULO, A.K.A. BO MA-MATAUKA

Who Is This Woman?

She was born as Wabei Lisulo, the firstborn daughter of Bo Ndate Wabei and Bo Ma-Wabei. Her father, Bo Ndate Wabei, was called Lisulo Musialela, the son of Musialela and Mukwae (Princess) Mwangala Ilitongo of the Barotse Royal Establishment in Barotseland, the western part of present Zambia. Mwangala was the daughter of Mombotwa and Mukatimui. Wabei Lisulo's mother was Bo Wamusheke, the daughter of Bo Ndate Monde and Bo Ma Monde from Nasikena village, Sefula. Bo Ndate Monde was later baptized as John and also popularly known as Abraham. Wamusheke's mother was Bo Ma-Monde (Bo Mukatimui).

Bo Wabei Lisulo, a.k.a. Bo Ma Matauka, born at Sefula ninety-two years earlier, started her primary education at Sefula (PEMS), completed her upper primary education at Mabumbu Girls' Boarding School (PEMS), and became a teacher by profession. Bo Ma-Wabei and Bo Ndate Wabei had five children together, four daughters and one son (Bo Wabei-Bo Ma-Matauka, Mwangala-Bo Ma-Victor, Bo Daniel Muchiwa Lisulo, Bo Muteletwa Bo Ma-Mukatimui, and Bo Mwangala-Ma-Lisulo).

Bo Wabei was blessed with seven children: Matauka, Wamusheke, Rose Kashembe, Sibeso, Namatama, Mwangelwa, and Watae. Bo Wabei had nineteen grandchildren and several great-grandchildren. At her demise in 2018, she was survived by four daughters, Bo Matauka, Bo Wamusheke, Bo Rose Kashembe and Sibeso.

Professional Career:
Teaching, Home Economics, and Politics

Bo Wabei Lisulo, a.k.a. Bo Ma-Matauka, obtained a primary teacher certificate and started teaching at Barotse National School (BNS), Kambule in Mongu, Barotseland, later known as Barotse Province but now called Western Province of Zambia. She also taught on the Copperbelt at Wusakile in Kitwe. Among her colleagues at Wusakile were the late vice president, Right Honorable Simon Mwansa Kapwepwe; Mrs. Salome Kapwepwe; Mrs. Namaya Mbikusita Lewanika (later became Imwambo, queen of the Litunga Mbikusita Lewanika 11).

From Wusakile, Kitwe, together with her husband, Mr. Daniel Fwanyanga Mukoboto, she went to study in India, where she pursued her further studies between 1955 and 1956. In India, she was among the two hundred African students sponsored in preparation for the liberation of the African continent. She studied home economics in Mumbai (then referred to as Bombay) and in New Delhi. While in Mumbai, she obtained an advanced certificate/diploma in home economics. She was also a freedom fighter who studied alongside other Zambian colleagues in Mumbai. Among them were five distinguished Zambian freedom fighters, namely:

- Late former vice president, the Right Honorable Simon Mwansa Kapwepwe

- Late former prime minister, the Right Honorable Mundia Nalumino
- Late former cabinet minister in Kenneth Kaunda's cabinet, Honorable Munukayumbwa Sipalo
- Mr. Mushashu Mushashu, who was among the first one hundred Zambian university graduates at Zambia's independence
- Mr. Pelekelo Musole, also among the first one hundred Zambian university graduates at independence

Bo Wabei Lisulo (Bo Ma-Matauka) was in the same program with the late former vice president, Right Honorable Simon Mwansa Kapwepwe, while the other four Zambians were pursuing different bachelor degrees.

In India, the two hundred African students from all over the African continent based in various locations of India were visited by the leading Pan-Africanists, including the late former president of South Africa, Mr. Nelson Mandela, and the late former president of Ghana, Dr. Kwame Nkrumah. At this stage in her life, our mother recalled significant interactions with African students from Tanzania, Kenya, Uganda, Ethiopia, Ghana, Nigeria, South Africa, Malawi, and Zimbabwe from whom she learned a lot, exchanging views about the struggle for independence and the Pan-Africanist sentiments of the time. She returned to Zambia in 1956, well-versed with the political ideas of the time and the need for political independence.

Upon her return to her home country, Zambia, she continued with her teaching career. She taught in Lusaka and then went back to teach at the Barotse National School (BNS) Kambule in Mongu; taught at Limulunga, Mangango/Kaoma, Lwatile, and Malengwa; and worked as a home economics organizer over a selected number of schools in Barotseland/Western Province. She was also amongst the teachers at Lwatile, serving as the school for Lealui Royal Palace, Litunga's summer capital, known to be the political activists against the colonial rule.

There was a memorable day when our home was searched as they were looking for her because she was a voice among women who spoke publicly against Welensky's government (the Federation of Rhodesia and Nyasaland). Despite the opposition, our mother continued to speak publicly for self-determination and self-black rule.

Bo Ma-Matauka's Spiritual Heritage at Sefula

Her spiritual heritage can be traced back to Sefula where she was born in Nasikena village and where she received her early education and socialization. Sefula is of special significance in her life since it was the very first PEMS station. During her teaching profession, Bo Ma-Matauka continued to serve God as a gospel minister in the marketplace. She was a psalmist, a worshipper, an evangelist, and a church planter.

Born at Sefula, her mother and father, our grandparents, were at the time ambassadors to Northwestern Zambia, with the headquarters being Zambezi (Luvale/Lubale). Until her demise, our grandmother always went to Chitokoloki mission for her dental checkups.

Her father was the ambassador for the Barotse Royal Establishment (BRE) to Northwestern Zambia. He served as the English/Lozi interpreter for the BRE and the royal courts. He had also studied at Sefula, where he met his wife, our grandmother, from Nasikena village, Sefula. My grandmother was one of the daughters to the three brothers who received François Coillard and helped him fix his tent on arrival in Sefula in 1884.

Her father, Bo Ndate Wabei, our grandfather, was also the chief royal translator and interpreter during the discussions and negotiations for the 1964 Barotseland Agreement, including negotiations at Lancaster House in London.

The father and mother to Bo Wabei Lisulo.

That was the period when then-Litunga Imutakwandu Sir Mwanawina 111 (Lewanika) signed the Barotseland Agreement with the first prime minister and later first president of Zambia, Dr. Kenneth Kaunda, on behalf of Barotseland. Among the Barotse delegates/dignitaries were Imutakwandu Mbikusita Lewanika 11, who became litunga after his brother, Sir Mwanawina 111. Sir Mwanawina 111 was knighted due to his courage as the then-royal prince who fought for both Northwestern and Northeastern Rhodesia during the Second World War. Sir Mwanawina 111 also studied at Sefula Normal School before pursuing higher education in South Africa. So did his elder brothers, Yeta 111 and Imwiko 1, and younger brother, Mbikusita Lewanika 11. They all went through Sefula before going to study abroad.

The Barotse Royal Establishment (BRE) at Lancaster House for discussions on the Barotse Agreement in May 1964 for Zambia to attain her independence as a unitary state.

Her Mother's Legacy: Nasikena Village and Sefula Mission

Sefula mission.

Wabei Lisulo and Her Brother, Daniel

Our mother had a younger brother named Daniel. He was born and named Muchiwa by his father. However, as soon as his Christian maternal uncles from Nasikena village in Sefula, Nehemiah Munalula and Eliezer Sikatana, arrived to visit the family, they renamed him Daniel. This was a prophetic act, as in the Bible. These uncles from Sefula had understood the power in a name. This is how immense the impact of missionary work and power of the gospel on a people or nation can get. Daniel was a Lozi University graduate, one among the first one hundred at independence. He had also been schooled at Sefula, where the Christian missionaries had shaped him into a strong leader.

The effect of the fire started at Sefula mission station continued to raze the entire nation as a good number of university graduates on the post-independence cabinet under Dr. Kenneth Kaunda's (KK's) rule were highly educated Lozis. They had all been trained and fashioned through Sefula Mission School established by the PEMS.

Daniel Lisulo rose in the Zambian government to the position of prime minister in KK's UNIP government. As prime minister, he was head of the Zambian government. He distinguished himself as a leader with a spirit of excellence, wisdom, and courage. These aspects of his character and work ethic were highly noticeable in his public life and manifested in the way he crafted his last will and testament, just as in Daniel 6:3, "Now Daniel so distinguished himself among the administrators and the satraps by his exceptional qualities that the king planned to set him over the whole kingdom."

When Daniel died in August 2000, *The Times of Zambia* featured his story as the "story of the week," titled "Lisulo, the Man of Excellence passes away." Daniel was among the first one hundred Zambian graduates at independence and among the first five Zambian lawyers and practitioners. He was the first Zambian to be honored as state counsel (SC) in Zambia.

Wabei with her late brother, later former prime minister of Zambia and state counsel, Mr. Daniel Muchiwa Lisulo, and her late cousin, Mwanang'ono Kufekisa Mbikusita Lewanika (photo), the firstborn son of King Mbikusita Lewanika 11.

Imbuwa Sikatana

CHAPTER 5

LESSONS FROM MY MOTHER

Lesson on Faith

Bo Ma-Matauka was a woman of incredible faith, and she believed and embraced the Word of God concerning her daughters. She raised the girl-child at a time when people were giving priority to sending their boys/sons to school. She was confident that her daughters were a gift from God despite not having done any gender studies. She had encountered a Bible story about Caleb's daughters who became heirs to their father's estate in a culture that allowed only men to do so (Joshua 15:13–19, 17:3–6). Caleb's daughters received more than expected, demonstrating the goodness of God and following a request to consider them. They were allotted a double portion. Similarly in Numbers 27, the five daughters of Zelophehad also made their inheritance claim before Moses, who took it before the Lord. Their request was considered favorably, and the people instituted a new regulation to secure their inheritance. The new law of inheritance changed to include families where there were only daughters and no sons in Numbers 27:6–8 (NLT)

And the Lord replied to Moses, "The claim of the daughters of Zelophehad is legitimate. You must give them a grant of land along with their father's relatives. Assign them the property that would have been given to their father. And give the following instructions to the people of Israel: If a man dies and has no son, then give his inheritance to his daughters."

Our mother had unwavering faith in God and His plan for her family. Even on the material day that our dad died, Mum was away attending a home economics refresher course. When the news was brought to her early Sunday morning, she was busy serving in the Lord's house, singing hymns, and ringing the church bell at Mabumbu PEMS mission school, calling people to worship.

My mother, Bo Wabei Lisulo, and my father,
Bo Daniel Fwanyanga Mukoboto, in 1948.

In those days, our father was considered a well-to-do man who took very good care of his family. He was also a very generous man. His generosity, hard work, excellent communication skills, leadership, and management skills were exemplary. Having worked for the Central African Mail, running multiple businesses with great entrepreneurial thinking and outstanding in leadership and management skills, he was called to go and help the then-Litunga (king), Sir Mwanawina 111 (Lewanika) and take a leading role in the administration and management of the affairs of the BRE. Unfortunately, he died mysteriously and never lived to see the fruit of his work. However, my father was a man who had voiced out his dreams for his children, and our mother always reminded us of the vision he had for us, his daughters.

Lessons on Love and Compassion

We witnessed our mother's love for God and fellow man through her dedicated service, the way she treated and took care of people, but more so through her positive outlook toward the downtrodden, the orphaned, the widows, the aged, and the vulnerable whom she took care of. She would often send her own children to step out to help the vulnerable with chores such as fetching water, preparing meals, washing clothes, cleaning their houses, and ensuring their environment was hygienic. She "adopted" several children, seeing them through school at her own cost at every school where she taught.

Lessons on Obedience

Our mother obeyed God and honored her parents. She loved and cared for them until they all died at a ripe old age. The honor she gave to her earthly parents earned her respect and honor from her relatives, neighbors, and the many children she had adopted.

Lessons on Loving God and His Word

Bo Ma-Matauka ensured that in her home, family devotion included all the family members. Even the little children were taught to read the Bible, pray, make presentations based on the Bible, and engage in evangelism, lay preaching, and discipleship. She valued true worship and praising God, our Creator. She told the stories and taught about "the obedient first missionaries" who brought the gospel to Bulozi/Barotseland and how they moved around sharing the gospel despite passing through dangerous locations with only the Bible as their weapon.

Testimony by Her Second-born Daughter, Bo Wamusheke

Bo Wamusheke, second-born daughter of Bo Ma-Matauka.

Bo Wamusheke, her second-born daughter, testified of how our mother possessed strong, deep faith that caused her to depend on God throughout her life. Even after losing her husband, our mother undoubtedly believed that God would take care of her and her children.

Lessons on Service to God and Mankind

Bo Wamusheke further observed that our mother was always available to serve in different roles at the church. During the planning, setting of the foundation, and construction of the family community church, now called Malengwa UCZ Congregation Church, our mother spent most of her day at the site. Her meals had to be delivered to her, and whatever was sent had to be sufficient to feed all the workers on site. Our mother loved people, particularly the vulnerable. There were occasions when Mum would give away her dinner to some hungry person, claiming that, after all, she was still fed from her lunch meal. Giving was her lifestyle.

One of her most favorite activities was engaging in Bible quizzes. This became a favorite too for the local community church. She studied her Bible, meditated on the Word, and thus was able to share and respond to various issues raised by the younger generation. Most people liked joining her group because they were always inspired by her eagerness to study the Word, meditate, ask questions, and cross-reference. Her Bible study group was always the liveliest. Our mother kept her Bible in very good condition, covering it with neat cloth cover, which she personally handmade.

She was a leader who depended on the guidance of the Holy Spirit, even to the planting of the local community church. She led by example and rallied both men and women to arise and do their part in the construction of the church to the glory of God. She was a lay preacher who served in the local church and other churches as a psalmist and evangelist. She sometimes shared the Word of God during church services. Our mother believed that God would be faithful to provide all that was needed to complete the local community church, which she planted, and it was so.

Lessons on Establishing a Strong Family Altar

Our mother always exalted God. She established a family altar in the home where all those present would gather in the evening to share the Word of God and worship. Our mother woke us up in the morning by singing one of her favorite hymns, "*Mulena lwa kubata*," translated into "Lord, we seek you at dawn before the sun rises as the night fades away; we ask for your grace and mercy and power and peace that flows from your throne."

This was a wake-up call for us, and we knew it was time to wake up and say our morning devotionals and prayers before going out. She would remind us to never step out into the world unarmed, not consulting God first daily. She did not have to knock on our doors. We just knew when she sung her song out loud that it was time to wake up and worship the Lord. Each one of us was given a role to play during the construction of the community church. In her final parting shot, the words she spoke to us before her death, was an instruction that we should not forget to renovate the house of the Lord whenever we took care of our other village homes. She instructed us to embrace true worship as the posture of our hearts. She encouraged us to worship God in spirit and in truth, for who He is, for what He has already accomplished on the cross, and for what He is doing and will continue to do in our lives. She urged us to live according to Micah 6:8, "to walk humbly with God," and taught us that true worship is being "a living and holy sacrifice which is acceptable to God" based on Romans 12:1–2.

> Therefore, I urge you, brothers, and sisters, in view of
> God's mercy, to offer your bodies as a living sacrifice,

holy and pleasing to God—this is your true and proper worship. Do not conform to the pattern of this world but be transformed by the renewing of your mind. Then you will be able to test and approve what God's will is—His good, pleasing, and perfect will.

Lessons to Trust God's Faithfulness

Bo Ma-Matauka, our mother, recognized God's faithfulness through her life. She diligently expounded on scriptures during our regular family devotions in the mornings and evenings as we were growing up. She shared with others while playing out her role as an evangelist, psalmist, minister in the marketplace, schoolteacher, community leader, and church planter. Referencing Psalm 45:1–21, Mum always exalted God as king and praised His name for His faithfulness. Mum placed emphasis on Psalm 45:4, on how each generation should tell its children of His mighty acts and proclaim His power through regular home devotions in the evening and morning glory sessions. She pointed out to her children life instances that revealed God's faithfulness and specific Bible promises where God demonstrates the fulfillment of His promises. We marveled at how faithfully God fulfilled promises to Abraham in giving him Isaac, the son of promise; how God had raised Joseph to be a prime minister in Egypt; and how He had delivered David from his enemies time and time again.

These biblical truths made Mum faithful to what she was entrusted with. She stood on these promises, and Mum shared testimonies of God's goodness in her life and the promises that God fulfilled in her life from her growing up, going to school, in her marriage, as a mother, and work life; how she excelled in her studies in India; and her return home to Zambia and her life with her children. In this testimonial book, we explore how faithful God has been. Our goal in honoring our mother is to honor God who makes all things possible.

God endowed our mother with the gifts of faith (Thumelo), hope (Sepo/Tsepo), love (Lilato/Lerato), obedience (Tundamo), and a deep love for the Word of God. Mum demonstrated and manifested these truths in her life.

Mum demonstrated the faith from God in her life. Whether in the valley or on the mountain, she believed in her God being with her. Mum understood faith as described in Hebrews 11:1–3. According to her, the elders of old, Abraham, Isaac, Jacob, Joseph, and David, obtained a good testimony because of their faith. She believed that their lives demonstrated and illustrated what genuine growing faith was and particularly how they worked out their faith and grew in it daily to the glory of God, how the faith of these elders of old lay hold of God's promises and the realities of unseen world. They applied these realities to their family lifestyles. Sometimes they fell short, but they kept holding to what their God had promised. She taught us how important it was for us to understand the nature of enduring faith.

Parenting Children with Eternity in Mind

No matter who we are, where we live, or what our goals may be, we all have one thing in common: we have a heritage passed on from our biological or spiritual parent to the next generation. Every one of us is lined up for a heritage, lives out a heritage, and gives a heritage to family, community, and the next generation. God has made it in such a way that we all pass on a legacy from our generation and to the next generation, good, bad, or a combination of both.

As Christians, we must intentionally pass on a legacy consistent with our Christian beliefs to the next generation. Failing to do so means that someone else will do it, but what gets passed on is beyond our control. We therefore need to take charge over that assignment. The current media and culture are busy influencing worldly beliefs, many of which may be contrary to our faith. It is therefore important for us to remember that passing on a positive legacy is a process we must engage in. We are responsible for the outcomes; thus, we cannot slacken or relegate the bringing up of our children to social media and other channels of this fallen world.

Christian adults and Christian parents who successfully pass along a spiritual legacy to the next generation model and reinforce the unseen realities of the godly life that our Creator expects of them. As Christians, we must recognize that passing a spiritual legacy means more than just encouraging our children to attend church or just driving them to the church entrance every Sunday and/or every Saturday, leaving them there, and expecting someone else to do the job for us. While that is important, it is only a preliminary step. At the local church, the Sunday school teacher is there to support parents in raising their children but cannot carry out the actual work that only parents and guardians can. Our mother was well aware of her role; thus, she managed to leave behind the spiritual legacy she desired as a Christian parent. She did this through various approaches:

- She acknowledged Jesus as her personal Savior and reinforced this through regular devotions at home, acknowledging God's sovereignty in all her actions and daily deeds.
- She practiced praying and living by faith as a lifestyle, a routine in life.
- She taught her children the Word and clarified what was grey. She encouraged us to study the Word and worship in song from an early age.
- The spiritual principles she taught had to be practiced at home, school, play, and daily living, as in "*Seli la luna*" (*Seli Laluna likanye kwa batu kaufela, alu ka sebeza zende balumbe Mulimu*). May our light shine so people come to the saving knowledge of Jesus Christ as Lord and Savior.
- She took the responsibility to transfer the truth and values God had given her to us, her children and grandchildren, as a personal obligation.

- She was purpose-driven to not only run and finish her life race well, but to also pass on the faith baton successfully to her children and grandchildren. Running to win the prize means we must pass on the truth and life of Christ deposited in us to the next generation.
- She lived out her faith with transparency and integrity and rubbed on godly character to her children, grandchildren, and brethren around her.

1 Seli la luna li kanye
li bonwe kwa batu
Ha lu ta sebeza ze nde
Ba lumbe Mulimu
Chorus Lu be linaleli
Ze nga liseli ku Jesu
Lu be mataseli
ka liseli la Jesu.
2 Ha lu kopani ni Jesu (lu sabe)
lu sabe ze maswe,
Mwa pilu ya ka niya hao
ku ine ze kenile
Chorus Lu be linaleli etc.
3 Kono ku ~~toona~~ swana ni wena
Jesu a lu boni
Tusa lu ine ku wena
ka nako kaufela
Chorus Lu be linaleli.

Bo Ma-Matauka's own handwritten version of the song, "Seli La luna likanye" (May our light shine like a sunbeam that draws its light from Jesus Christ).

Our mother purposely left spiritual blessings in our lives as her children and among her grandchildren. She did this whenever we gathered at her residence, utilizing every opportunity, or when she visited our homes. She would intentionally spend quality time with her grandchildren to pass on these eternal truths in simple, fun ways.

When my daughter Lucy was in lower grade at an international school, she was taught about the message of "the cross" and found it very confusing. However, when my mother visited us, she simplified this for the little girl, and soon they were both joyfully singing aloud, "I am not ashamed of the cross." While Mum sang it in her language, Silozi, my young daughter, sang it in English. She later performed the same song in class when the teacher asked students to share their favorite songs from their own homes.

Lucy sang, "I am not ashamed of the cross, at the cross, at the cross." My mother sang it in Lozi. "*Ani swabi kubulelela ya nza a ni pilisa, nitumise Bizo lahae aninze ni pila.*"

By the time of her death in February 2018, her four adult daughters were diligently serving God in the marketplace. They are also striving to raise children who will be likewise committed to raising their children to follow God wholeheartedly. This does not just happen by chance, but requires parents to love children enough to train them in God's ways, instill godly character in them, discipline them with love, instruct them in God's Word, and teach them to pray and to live for God for the rest of their lives. Our God is generational.

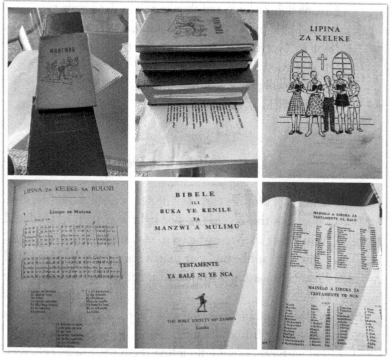

Bo Ma-Matauka's Silozi *Bibele Ye Kenile, Sifela ni Munembo*
(Holy Bible, hymn book, and melody/songbook).

The Joy of Serving God and Others

For Mum, the seemingly never-ending effort paid off. The single most important legacy we can leave is our children serving the Lord and thereby affecting their generation and thereafter and remembering the quality of our life in Christ has a major influence upon our children, the current generation, and the next generation. In Mum, we saw evidence that godly living has eternal value, impacting life both now and the life to come. She shone the light of Jesus to her children and the local community where she lived, letting the light of her Christian faith shine forth before people in the good deeds that she performed.

No one lights a lamp and then puts it under a basket. Instead, a lamp is placed on a stand, where it gives light to everyone in the house. In the same way, let your good deeds shine out for all to see, so that everyone will praise your heavenly Father. (Matthew 5:15–16 NLT)

A Legacy of Good Deeds

Through her acts of kindness and loving service, she would say that her prayer was that those who saw her light may turn to God and begin to "praise our Father in heaven." "A sunbeam, a sunbeam, Jesus wants me for a sunbeam," our mother sang and demonstrated it. "*Lube Linaleli zenga Liseli Ku Jesu, Lu be Mataseli. Ka Liseli La Jesu.*"

She also loved and practiced *Sikundi* (word originating from her people in harvesting fish and fruits), evangelizing and sharing the Word of God with others, and discipling them to grow as believers. She lived by Proverbs 11:30, "he who wins souls is wise," and Daniel 12:3, "those who lead many to righteousness, will shine like the stars for ever and ever!"

Winning souls for Christ was important for her because she knew her God well and understood her influence in leading someone to the saving faith in Jesus Christ had an impact on their present life and through to eternity. She made us understand that the moment someone got saved, they received an inheritance of eternal life. 2 John 1:1–2 (NLT) reads, "This letter is from John, the elder. I am writing to the chosen lady and to her children, whom I love in the truth—as does everyone else who knows the truth— because the truth lives in us and will be with us forever."

Investing in the Younger Generation

Mum impacted the lives of the younger generation, even those young enough to be her great-grandchildren. The church construction project and the wall fencing done at the Malengwa church she planted remained a classic example where the young people got motivated because of her commitment and actions demonstrated to the cause of sharing the gospel, church planting, and church growth. Such was the testimony of the youths during her funeral on February 21, 2018, who passionately told of how committed they were to complete the wall fence for the church because of the example set by an old woman at ninety-two who had faithfully left a rich legacy of completing her part of the wall fence. They were devoted to also doing their part to carry that forward.

This was putting the Word into practice where an elder Christian looks for God-given opportunities to impart eternal truths into the lives of the younger generations around her. Mum also taught this through song to both her biological and spiritual children. She taught all of us to sing and pray scripture. In this case, she taught us to internalize scripture from a very young age through song. This is a very effective method of teaching the Bible to children and societies that are semi-literate in the written scripts and today. Today when we meet as siblings, we still remember the verses she taught this way, such as Matthew 7:24–27 (NLT),

> Anyone who listens to my teaching and follows it is wise, like a person who builds a house on solid rock. Though the rain comes in torrents and the floodwaters rise and the winds beat against that house, it won't collapse because it is built on bedrock. But anyone who hears my teaching and doesn't obey it is foolish, like a person who builds a house on sand. When the rains and floods come and the winds beat against that house, it will collapse with a mighty crash.

When we meet as a family, we just remind each other with, "*Mutu ya yahile Ndu ya fa licwe ki yena ya ta kena kwa Halimu!*" This means, "Therefore, everyone who hears these words of mine and puts them into practice is like a wise man who built his house on the rock."

The Place of Songs of Worship

From a very early age, she and my grandmother would gather us as a family choir and sing scripture. Another favorite we still sing when we meet is based on true disciples, "*A ki batu kaufela ba bali kuna Mulena lubulela linzwi la hao.*" It is not everyone who says, "Lord, Lord, who will enter the kingdom of God?"

Matthew 7:21–23 (NLT) reads,

> "Not everyone who calls out to me, 'Lord! Lord!' will enter the Kingdom of Heaven. Only those who actually do the will of my Father in heaven will enter. On judgment day many will say to me, 'Lord! Lord! We prophesied in your name and cast out demons in your name and performed many miracles in your name.' But I will reply, 'I never knew you. Get away from me, you who break God's laws.'"

A muzwe kuna ani mi zibi!
"A good man leaves an inheritance for his children's children ..." (Proverbs 13:22). From Mum's story, we learn we can leave an enduring legacy in many ways, including:

- Influencing our children and grandchildren to know and serve the Lord
- Living a godly life every waking hour
- Building our life and of those whom we influence upon the eternal word of God

- Letting our good deeds and the light-giving effect of living our Christian faith shine forth to touch the lives of those around us
- Winning souls for the Lord
- Touching the lives of our generation, the next generation, and of those even much younger than we are with the wisdom the Lord has given us over the years, purposely targeting to mentor younger people
- Loving and serving our local church with all our might
- Doing everything in our God-given grace and power as beacons of truth and blessing to our community

Mum was God-fearing and obeyed God. Her legacy began in her own heart, in her intimate relationship with God, which she demonstrated in her daily living to her children. Psalm 112:1–3 (NLT) reads, "Praise the Lord! How joyful are those who fear the Lord and delight in obeying his commands. Their children will be successful everywhere; an entire generation of godly people will be blessed. They themselves will be wealthy, and their good deeds will last forever."

Mum responded positively to her community's needs with compassion and action. By sharing the good news of the gospel of our Lord Jesus Christ, serving her people, and planting a church. In Matthew 9:36, we read, "And seeing the multitudes. He [Jesus] felt compassion for them." Our mother had a passion for winning souls as an evangelist through Sikundi and church planting. Mum leaves a legacy because she acted with courage to reach out to the lost and those in need.

Mum made prayer a priority, and she knew God would use her to accomplish His purposes. As Jabez prayed in 1 Chronicles 4:10 (NLT), "He was the one who prayed to the God of Israel, 'Oh, that you would bless me and expand my territory! Please be with me in all that I do and keep me from all trouble and pain!' And God granted him his request." Mum prayed that God would enlarge her territory spiritually, and God granted her request. During her last two years and five months of her life and at her send-off, the people of

Mongu, the Western Province, others from Lusaka, the capital city of Zambia, and various Christian denominations and different walks of life showed up in throngs, everyone eager to share their testimony of how she had impacted their lives.

Mum strived to be a faithful steward to her God-given talents, gifts, and abilities. She recognized this through her mother, father, uncles, and grandparents, whom God had used to extend His kingdom. She served others, taught the scripture, evangelized, and demonstrated in very practical ways how to live as a daughter of the Most High God. She was a minister in the marketplace, a lay preacher, and a leader with a vision for her community. She planted a church on her own father's land, at the royal village that stands to date. This was also where her send-off was held when she went to be with the Lord in February 2018.

Mum sought God's purpose and approval. Equally, she asked God to give her children a sense of purpose, direction, and mission. She strove toward leaving her children a heritage and not just an inheritance. She taught us that vision and divine direction in life were most significant. In essence, true vision, direction, and destiny can come only from God, for He is the One who controls the past, the present, and the future. Mum discovered her eternal destiny, and from this basis, she built a purposeful life while setting Jesus as the standard in her home.

CHAPTER 6

FAITH, HOPE, AND LOVE

Bo Ma-Matauka Exemplified the Enduring Principles of Faith, Hope, and Love

"And now abide faith, hope, love, these three; but the greatest of these is love" (1 Corinthians 13:13).

Our mother not only recognized the enduring principles of faith, hope, and love, but she also allowed her life and Christian walk to be governed by these foundational pillars. The Bible clearly states, "Without faith it is impossible to please God" (Hebrews 11:6). We grew up around a mother who trusted God and closely related with Him. She was fully aware that the God she served was the one true living God. She could count on His Word and trust in His faithfulness, and this compelled her to love Him in return. Her relationship with God led her to devoted obedience and diligent service through practicing acts of love and kindness to those around her. She loved God with all her heart, mind, and soul and strived to love her fellow human beings in any way she could.

Growing up, we witnessed her facing many difficult situations courageously with a deep understanding that God always relates to us in love, even when He allows us to encounter a difficult situation in life. One of those difficult seasons was when our dad died. Mum never complained or faltered in her faith; she kept hope alive that God would establish our family despite the difficulties. She also spoke to her children and reminded us to keep on trusting in God, believing in His Word, depending on Him as our provider, and to never forget God still loved us and was with us. Losing a father at a young age is a very significant event in any child's life. For my family, losing our father so early in life meant significant adjustments in our lifestyle, taking on new responsibilities and a whole new role for our mother as the head of our home.

I recall days when we would sneak into her room and find her on her knees in passionate prayer. We would watch her for a while as she modeled the way for us, the way of calling on the name of Jehovah. The moment she would emerge from that prayer closet, she would be exuding such confidence, and laughter would be ringing in her voice. She would be radiant in joyful countenance. This was her way of tapping into divine strength to face whatever challenges lay ahead of her. She excelled in taking good care of us, and the Lord was her support. We never were in need. There was enough food for every day despite having many visitors in our home. We never went hungry, we had a good shelter, we attended school, and our fees were paid despite us being a bunch of girls concurrently at school. It was at a time when girls were not prioritized to receive formal education. Our home had this amazing atmosphere that cannot be easily described in words. We witnessed Mum putting God's Word into practice, we saw her draw nearer to God through prayer, and we experienced God's presence and pleasures in the way He provided for our family. We learned and realized that we "must believe that He is and that He is a rewarder of those who seek Him" (Hebrews 11:16).

The Outcomes of My Mother's Faith

"Faith is the confidence that what we hope for will actually happen; it gives us assurance about things we cannot see" (Hebrews 11:1).

Through Faith, the Spiritual Becomes Real

When our mum spoke about her God, it was with such a deep level of confidence, leaving no doubt in us that God was our Father and provider of all we needed, while she was the noble vessel God chose to use to accomplish this. As a nine-year-old girl-child, I was impacted for life with an assurance in what God can do. My mother's faith established confidence and trust in me toward her God. Through Mum, I began to understand how faith gave substance to what is promised. Through her faith, there was evidence of what she believed in and about unseen and hoped-for realities. Through her, I saw a faith-strewn path to viewing my future while in my present and the experience of seeing the invisible. Through her walk of faith, she was able to demonstrate to me, her daughter, that the things we presently cannot see in the natural sense—God, angels, heaven, and hell—are as real as they get in the realm of the spirit. This brought me to my knees in surrender to His rule in my life, and as a young girl, I accepted Jesus Christ as my personal Savior and Lord. Through her walk of faith, I saw the future promises of God brought to my own present focus. Faith enables us to see the unseen spiritual world the natural eye cannot.

Bo Ma-Matauka and her mother, my grandmother, animatedly told us the stories of courageous men of faith in the Bible. Sometimes the lessons were brought home through song as we sang songs in Silozi about Daniel, King Belshazzar, and the writing on the wall.

Ne kuna ni Mulena Ya Bizwa Belshazar, Ya na ezize mukiti wa kuca ni wa kunwa, mwahala busihu mwa Kashandi kahae atahelwa kimakazo lizoho fa limota!

Zoho lahae lang'ola, zoho lahae la ng'ola batu bote
bakomoka mi Mulena angangangama a babona zoho
la ng'ola!

Their narratives were given in such vivid animation style that they stuck. It was hard to forget the songs. "*Batangana Ba Ma-Heberu*" was about the three Hebrew boys, Shadrach, Meshach, and Abednego, in Daniel 3, who braved the fiery furnace in Babylon. They were young but demonstrated such great faith in Yahweh. Their courageous answer to a furious king oozes with faith in the unseen God.

> O Nebuchadnezzar, we do not need to give you an answer concerning this matter. If it be so, our God whom we serve is able to deliver us from the furnace of blazing fire; and He will deliver us out of your hand, O king. But even if He does not, let it be known to you, O king, that we are not going to serve your gods or worship the golden image that you have set up. (Daniel 3:16—18)

Our mother, through her lifestyle, encouraged us to embrace enduring faith in a big God, the kind of faith that opens the eyes of men to realize spiritual reality.

Faith Receives God's Commendation

"Through their faith, the people in days of old
earned a good reputation" (Hebrews 11:2).

Through the daily evening devotions by the fireside in our home, Mum told us stories and drew biblical lessons for us. She taught us scriptural songs to deepen the truth. I remember one of them, the "Nicodemus Song."

There was a man, A Pharisee named Nicodemus
the Ruler of the Jews, he came to Jesus by Night,
and he wanted to know more about the Kingdom
of God, one, two, God is going to take our troubles
away ...

From such a song, she would emphasize the deeper meaning of
salvation through Jesus Christ and what it means to be "born again."
She would also insist on the importance of *Sikundi*, evangelizing
to the lost souls in obedience to God's command. She would also
share about the kingdom of God and how to first seek it. "Seek the
Kingdom of God above all else, and live righteously, and He will give
you everything you need" (Matthew 6:33).

These are approaches to outreach that have worked every time
and should not be abandoned as they provide simple ways to better
internalize the Word of God within cultural context with greater
impact.

Mom placed emphasis on the need to seek God's approval in
whatever we do. "For by faith the men of old gained approval," with
a clear implication that the approval came from God. We learned
that if we put our faith in Jesus Christ and leave the conversion to
Him, He will save all those who come to Him in faith from eternal
damnation, "*Thumelo, ni Tsepo, ni Lirato, kono ye tuna kuzona ki
Lerato!*" translating into "Faith, hope, and love, but the greatest of
them all is love." These simplified lessons about faith and trust in
God, about salvation through faith and by the grace of God, trusting
Jesus as our personal Savior and Lord, we got to appreciate the need
to live each day in obedience (Tundamo), seeking His approval for
His glory because "without faith it is impossible to please Him" (11:6).
We got to learn that faith is the means of realizing spiritual reality
and gaining God's approval.

Faith As the Means of Understanding
the Origin of All That Is

"It is by faith we understand that the whole world was
made by God's command so what we see was made by
something that cannot be seen" (Hebrews 11:3).

Our mother did not leave it up to us children to believe whatever we
wanted to believe about creation or our identity; instead, she pointed
us to Elohim, the eternal Creator of all. She focused her family to look
to the mighty one who spoke to nothing, and that nothing became
something (matter created from nothing; invisible made visible).
Many parents today are leaving their children to believe in whatever
they may, but not so with Bo Ma-Matauka. She introduced to us the
truth and reinforced it through the Silozi books of the Bible song
"*Gexelenudejo Barusasamama ...*" We gained an understanding of the
fact that it is by faith that we understand how the universe (and time)
came into being, simply through God's spoken Word. The eternal
God brought physical matter and time into being by His powerful
Word alone! We can only understand that by faith, and that faith in
God as Creator is foundational to knowing Him. "In the beginning
God created the heavens and the earth" (Genesis 1:1a).

We cannot begin to understand ourselves as a people or fathom
the world history or God Himself until we apply faith. Even more
important is to believe in His Word about His free gift of salvation.
Only then can we gain an understanding about the origins of the
ages that cause everything in history to fall into place. God desires
that all people know Him through faith that endures trials to the
preservation of the soul (Hebrews 10:39). This kind of faith takes
the future promises of God and makes them real in the present. It
proves the reality of the unseen world. It gains God's approval. It
understands the origins of all that is. As Hebrews 11 details, this
kind of faith is outright simple and practical. It is the kind of faith
that has sustained the people of God through thousands of years in
every sort of difficulty. It is the faith that sustained our mother, Bo

Ma-Matauka, that continues to sustain us in this season and in the future days to come.

This remarkable African mama was obedient to her calling and faithful to steward all she was entrusted with. She used the land she received from her paternal royal uncle and father to plant and erect a worship sanctuary. From this local church, the community has continued to worship God and connect with one another in Christ love. The local church she established is now recognized as the UCZ branch modeled on Sefula transformation ideals and is called Malengwa UCZ Church. Our mother left us with a challenge of what we must do with what God has given us in our hands that will impact His kingdom.

During her burial, there were passionate testimonies by the young people and youth who had been engaged in block-making about the amazing work and dedication to God's work she had displayed that had challenged them at the individual level to also give their best in kingdom work. Before she fell sick, the congregation had agreed to build a wall fence around the church, and the only part standing on February 21, 2018, during her burial was the section she had built to the glory of God. This led me to reflect on Hebrews 10:23–24 (NLT), "Let us hold tightly without wavering to the hope we affirm, for God can be trusted to keep his promise. Let us think of ways to motivate one another to acts of love and good works."

And in thinking of our mother's legacy, I was reminded of Deuteronomy 7:9 (NLT), "Understand, therefore, that the Lord your God is indeed God. He is the faithful God who keeps his covenant for a thousand generations and lavishes his unfailing love on those who love him and obey his commands." It is our earnest desire as a family to follow in our mother's footsteps in walking in the ways of our Lord and Savior, Jesus Christ, and to teach our children to do so wholeheartedly.

The Outcomes of My Mother's Hope (Sepo/Tsepo)

The Hope of His Calling

Our mother, Bo Ma-Matauka, through the help of the Holy Spirit, understood the hope of God's calling on her own life, with clear knowledge of who she was in Him. She pursued an active knowledge of truth daily and embraced the hope that never disappoints. "And this hope will not lead to disappointment. For we know how dearly God loves us, because He has given us the Holy Spirit to fill our hearts with His love" (Romans 5:5 NLT).

Our mother stayed spiritually alert through prayer.

> Asking God, the glorious Father of our Lord Jesus Christ, to give you spiritual wisdom and insight so that you might grow in your knowledge of God. I pray that your hearts will be flooded with light so that you can understand the confident hope he has given to those he called—his holy people who are his rich and glorious inheritance. (Ephesians 1:17–18 NLT)

She treasured this scriptural prayer that presents hope as confident expectation, the sure certainty that what God has promised in His Word is true, must occur, and will occur in accordance with His Word. This hope is an indication of certainty and a strong and confident expectation that God will do what He said He would do and closely relates to faith. Just like the gift of faith, hope lays emphasis on the future and the invisible, things we have neither nor received, yet we lay hold of them through faith. "We were given this hope when we were saved. (If we already have something, we don't need to hope for it. But if we look forward to something we don't yet have, we must wait patiently and confidently)" (Romans 8:24–25 NLT).

Bo Ma-Matauka often sang, *"Fo ni tomela Sepo Kaufela Ki famali Ahao, Swaleleo Yaka; Bupilo bwaka, ki kuwena Jesu. Se ni lumela se nitabela, Ki Rato la Jesu; oh Mupulusi, ya na lushwezi, ni li ni be wa hao."* Indeed, our hope is an assurance grounded in the finished, redemptive work of Jesus Christ.

The Outcomes of My Mother's Love (Lerato/Lilato)

Bo Ma-Matauka's Definition of Biblical Love

Mum believed that love is the Word of God in action, often reminding us of God's love as told of in John 3:16 (NLT), "For this is how God loved the world: He gave his one and only Son, so that everyone who believes in him will not perish but have eternal life."

Apostle John in the first letter of John 4 elaborates on the fact that God is love, He loves us, and He resides in us; thus, we can also love as He does.

> We know how much God loves us, and we have put our trust in his love. God is love, and all who live in love live in God, and God lives in them. And as we live in God, our love grows more perfect. So, we will not be afraid on the day of judgment, but we can face him with confidence because we live like Jesus here in this world. We love each other because he loved us first. (1 John 4)

Mum Bo Ma-Matauka kept unwrapping unto her children the multidimensional nature of the love of God. She used local dialect phrases such as *"Buliba bwa Lerato Lahae, la Komosa,"* meaning that His love is so wide and deep that it is boundless, indescribable, marvelous, amazing, and too wonderful to comprehend. The word *buliba* means "in the deep," for one can never quite get to the end of the deep. Through songs, our mother taught us to sing and recite 1 Corinthians 13:1–13 (NLT) in Silozi, concluding with verse 13 as the chorus, "Three things will last forever—faith, hope, and love—and the greatest of these is love."

We sang of this amazing love both at home and the Sunday school, "This is my commandment that we love one another that our Joy may be full." She also told the story of how the Lord Jesus Christ responded to the Pharisees about what the greatest commandment was.

> Jesus replied, "You must love the Lord your God with all your heart, all your soul, and all your mind. This is the first and greatest commandment. A second is equally important: 'Love your neighbor as yourself.' The entire law and all the demands of the prophets are based on these two commandments." (Mathew 22:37–40 NLT).

Our mother loved people. Her home was frequented by both children and adults from all walks of life for short- or long-term stays. There were nephews, nieces, aunties, uncles, mothers, fathers, grandfathers, grandmothers, great-uncles, and great-aunties. Everyone was a welcomed guest and treated with honor. From her experience as a schoolteacher, many people who wanted to send their children to school requested she assist with their accommodation across the various schools where she taught. She made it clear to her own biological children that all these people who passed through her hands and lived in our home were important to God and we were to honor them. We dared not forget the names from the family tree and how we were related to the many people who had passed through her hands and found abode in our home.

A hospitable woman, she was such that meals were prepared with extra portion, available for guests who came by. None entered her home without having a meal placed before them, whether it was breakfast, lunch, or dinnertime. I recall being young and worrying whether the food would be enough to share among all those present, but with time, we realized that because of her faith in God, there was always enough food to go around and her family never went hungry or faced lack. Our generous mother, Bo Ma-Matauka, applied love, blended with faith in Jehovah Jireh, our provider, and He never once failed to meet all our needs. She practiced love in the biblical way, caring in action in obedience to the Word of God. She taught us that love is not what we just feel but what we do, as described in this verse, "Now that you have purified yourselves by obeying the truth so that you have sincere love of each other, love one another deeply, from the heart. For you have been born again, not of perishable seed, but of imperishable, through the living and enduring word of God" (1 Peter 1:22–23).

Peter further emphasizes this in making the Christians' calling and election sure in 2 Peter 1:5–7, where he admonishes Christians to make every effort to demonstrate these qualities, which include love. "For this very reason, make every effort to add to your faith goodness, and to goodness, knowledge; and to knowledge, self-control; and to self-control, perseverance; and to perseverance, godliness; And to godliness, mutual affection; and to mutual affection, LOVE." Peter accentuates that if Christians possess these qualities in increasing measure, they will be effective and productive in their lives.

Bo Ma-Matauka described this love to us in vivid terms, referring to Christ's death for our sins because of His love for us in that "but God demonstrates his own love for us in this: While we were still sinners, Christ died for us" (Romans 5:8).

Bo Ma-Matauka, our mum, also taught us love through *Sikundi*, casting out our nets as fishermen would reach others in communities outside her own home through evangelizing to the lost souls and discipling new converts to mature in faith. She was on the front line in giving service to others, extending practical love, and sharing what we had. She encouraged us to courageously share the good news of this love of God with others. She was very impatient with

CHAPTER 7

THE KEY OF OBEDIENCE

Obedience (Tundamo) Motivated by Love

According to *Holman's Illustrated Bible Dictionary*, a succinct definition of biblical obedience is "to hear God's Word and act accordingly." *Eerdmans Bible Dictionary* states that "true 'hearing,' or obedience, involves the physical hearing that inspires the hearer, and a belief or trust that in turn motivates the hearer to act in accordance with the speaker's desires." Thus, biblical obedience to God means to hear, trust, submit, and totally surrender to His Word. And this is what Bo Ma-Matauka, our mum, taught us.

Her calling was sure, and she strove to accomplish what God had called her to do. She always wanted the best for the congregants and looked out for the reverend and his family at the church she planted at Malengwa in Mongu. She ensured the reverend and his family were taken good care of and their needs adequately met. This was confirmed by the same reverend when he gave the eulogy at our mother's funeral. He gave many examples of how mum demonstrated God's love in action. Our mom emphasized the truth that Christians are called to obedience to God, with Jesus Christ being the perfect model of obedience. As his disciples, we are to follow Christ's example, living according to His commands, with our motivation for obedience being love. "If you love me, obey my commandments" (John 14:15 NLT).

Obedience Is an Act of Worship

Obedience is therefore an act of worship as we demonstrate recognition and gratitude for who God is. Our mother often played the song, "Thank You, Lord, for Your Blessings on Me," and emphasized her gratitude for the family the Lord had given her! Through her, we learned that true Christian obedience flows from a heart of gratitude for the grace and mercy we have received from the Lord. As Paul clearly states in Romans 12:1 (NLT), "And so, dear brothers and sisters, I plead with you to give your bodies to God because of all he has done for you. Let them be a living and holy sacrifice—the kind he will find acceptable. This is truly the way to worship Him."

Mum had a grateful spirit and always taught us to be grateful. She was ever grateful for the family, and this country-western gospel song was a favorite we played for her on her deathbed at ninety-two years old.

> *As the world looks upon me, as I struggle along,*
> *they say I have nothing, but they are so wrong*
> *In my heart I'm rejoicing, how I wish they could see,*
> *Thank you Lord, for your blessings on me*
> **Chorus**
> *There's a roof up above me, I've a good place to sleep*
> *There's food on my table, And shoes on my feet*
> *You gave me your love Lord, And a fine family*
> *Thank you, Lord, for your blessings on me*

Now I know I'm not wealthy, and these clothes, they're
not new,
I don't have much money, but Lord I have you
And to me that's all that matters, though the world
cannot see,
Thank you, Lord, for your blessings on me
—Tune by Jeff and Sheri Easter

God Rewards Obedience

In the book of James, we are instructed to put into practice what the Word says. James 1:22–25 (NLT) reads,

> But don't just listen to God's word. You must do what it says. Otherwise, you are only fooling yourselves. For if you listen to the word and don't obey, it is like glancing at your face in a mirror. You see yourself, walk away, and forget what you look like. But if you look carefully into the perfect law that sets you free, and if you do what it says and don't forget what you heard, then God will bless you for doing it.

And the Lord Jesus Christ in Luke 11: 24-26, while casting out a mute demon, also takes this opportunity in Luke 11:28 to teach us to put the Word of God into practice.

Obedience Is an Act of Service

The Bible instructs us to serve God and others. 1 Corinthians 10:31–33 (NLT) reads, "So whether you eat or drink, or whatever you do, do it all for the glory of God. Don't give offense to Jews or Gentiles or the church of God. I, too, try to please everyone in everything I do. I don't just do what is best for me; I do what is best for others so that many may be saved."

Colossians 3:23–24 commands us to work willingly at whatever we do, as though we were working for the Lord rather than for people. And that there is an eternal reward from the Lord. The Lord also expects us to use our gifts, talents, and resources to serve others, 1 Peter 4:10–11 (NLT) states,

> God has given each of you a gift from his great variety of spiritual gifts. Use them well to serve one another. Do you have the gift of speaking? Then speak as though God himself were speaking through you. Do you have the gift of helping others? Do it with all the strength and energy that God supplies. Then everything you do will bring glory to God through Jesus Christ. All glory and power to him forever and ever! Amen.

Mum always insisted on evangelizing and conducting *Sikundi* as an act of obedience to God through serving Him and serving people besides doing so through church planting.

Obedience Indicates We Love God

If we love God, we shall obey His commandments. 1 John 5:2–4 (NLT) states, "We know we love God's children if we love God and obey his commandments. Loving God means keeping his commandments, and his commandments are not burdensome. For every child of God defeats this evil world, and we achieve this victory through our faith."

Just like love, obedience is an action word of doing what God has commanded us to do. He has commanded us to love one another, and we do it, love one another. If we love one another, we share the gospel with the lost souls. We evangelize and diligently disciple others until they reach the stage where they can also evangelize and disciple others. We are sanctified through obedience through the Holy Spirit. When we obey and allow the Holy Spirit to infill and re-infill us, we grow spiritually, to become more and more like Christ. "Obedience is better than sacrifice." The posture of our heart must be that of obedience, which yields righteousness, peace, and joy in the Holy Spirit.

Obedience Rooted in God's Word

The way of faith, hope, love, and obedience can only be understood if we view it from the perspective of the Word of God. Establishing a family altar is important; so is conducting family devotions and sharing the Word at every opportune moment. Through teaching children well and how to meditate on the Word from the time they are young, they learn obedience. Bo Ma-Matauka, our mum, taught us about this during morning and evening devotions where each one of us was expected to read the Bible for themselves, explain what we understood, and do well in the Bible quizzes conducted on a regular basis. Through such ways, we were able to internalize the Word of God and value His commands. We came to appreciate

- The Word of God provides guidance, showing the way as a light does on how we should live.
- Psalm 119:105 (NLT) reads, "Your word is a lamp to guide my feet and a light for my path."
- Studying the Word of God helps us know God more and therefore align our thoughts with God and prepare us for better service, which is in line with His will.
- Meditating on the Word of God helps us understand the Trinity, the triune God, God the Father, God the Son, and God the Holy Spirit, and that when we can call upon Him, He hears and answers.

CHAPTER 8

MY MOTHER'S HOMEGOING

Testimonies During Mum's Illness: October 2015–February 2018

Our mother went to be with the Lord on Sunday evening of February 18, 2018, the month of Yowa in Silozi, at the good, ripe age of ninety-two. She was survived by four senior daughters. She had borne seven children, but three of them died before her. She suffered a mild stroke on Tuesday, September 29, 2015, and was admitted to Lewanika General Hospital.

I arrived in Lusaka from Windhoek, Namibia, on Friday, October 2, 2015. On Saturday morning, October 3, 2015, I called my elder sister, Bo Wamusheke, who informed me of Mum's deteriorating condition while at Lewanika General Hospital in Mongu, Western Province of Zambia. I had intended to purchase my bus ticket to travel on Sunday, October 4, 2015, but there was obvious urgency in my sister's voice. She advised that if I could, I should leave for Mongu the same day Saturday, October 3, 2015, and not wait for the Sunday bus. I did.

God Speaks and Backs Up
His Word to Perform It

Before leaving Lusaka for Mongu, I called the church leadership at Northmead Assembly of God Church and requested prayer over Mum's health and the long journey ahead of me. It was a road trip of more than 500 kilometers under poor road conditions. The church leadership led by Bishop Joshua Banda and his wife, Pastor Gladys Banda; Reverend and Mrs. Khatanga; Reverend and Mrs. Nyirenda; and Pastor and Mrs. Haggai Mweene stood with us in prayer. As we prayed, a word of knowledge came from the Lord through Reverend Khatanga that we should drive in peace as we would find Mum still alive, she would be with us for some time, and she would live to bless us before she finally goes to be with her Lord. We were highly encouraged and left for Mongu with this hope. We arrived safely in Mongu, went straight to Lewanika General Hospital, and found her still alive.

The Northmead Assembly of God (NAOG)
Church leadership who prayed (2015).

Early Sunday morning, October 4, 2015, instead of going to the local church, we gathered around her hospital bed, planning to conduct a church service there and to pray with her. When we got to her bedside, she instead was the one who started ministering to us through offering heartfelt worship and praise. She led us into singing the Redemption Hymn in the Silozi hymn book, Hymn 184, "*Muise Liseli*" (Send the Light).

She led the worship and then spoke to us from her sickbed, reminding us of the Great Commission; we were to go, share the light, make disciples, and teach the new converts, according to Matthew 28:18–20 and Mark 16:15–18. She also emphasized the instructions in Matthew 5:16 to be the light that shines in the darkness, seeking to rescue many lost souls for the kingdom of God. She further reminded us of the Macedonian call, which was very dear to her heart because she grew up at Nasikena village in Sefula. That was where the PEMS and the Basotho evangelists led by Reverend François Coillard established their first church on a transformational model in Bulozi/Barotseland. Having grown up in Nasikena village in Sefula, our mother and her family studied, applied, and lived by the book of Acts. The Macedonian call detailed in Acts 16 was one among many of her favorite passages. Bo Ma-Matauka loved the Word of God, and she loved this song.

1. Utwa taelo ya Mulena i li:	The Lord's command is to send the light
Mu ise liseli!	To fight for/defend the sinners.
Mu y'o lamulela baezalibi,	Send the light!
Mu ise liseli	
Mu iseze batu liseli	Take the light to the people.
Kai ni kai mwa lifasi	Everywhere in the world
Mu ise taba za bupilo	Take the Word of Life
Kwa batu ba mishobo	To all peoples, kindred, and language groups
2. Ki yo u nz'a li batu ba isezwe	There is our Lord saying take
Liseli, Liseli!	The light, the light!

Ki ba mwa Bulozi ba ba tokwile	People in Bulozi need
Liseli, Liseli!	The light, light

3. Mu ba utwele butuku, ni mina	Be merciful, compassionate, feel for them
Mu ise liseli!	Send the light
Ki lungu za Mulena ze timela,	They are the Lord's lost sheep.
Mu ise liseli	Send the light

4. Ha mu hana, mu ta buzwa ka bona	If you do not go, you will be accountable
Mu ise liseli!	Send the light!
Mu lumilwe, si ke mwa bilaela	You are instructed/sent, do not hesitate.
Mu ise liseli	Send the light

Bo Ma-Matauka's Hospitalization

Typical of Bo Ma-Matauka, the sole passionate plea from her heart to her children was that we arise and go forth to preach and share the good news about Jesus, echoed even from her sickbed. While we were gathered around her hospital bed, she shared a spiritual experience she was having right there and then. She could see many people from different nations praying for her. She specifically mentioned seeing the Northmead Assembly of God Church leadership in Lusaka, led by Bishop Joshua Banda and his wife, Pastor Gladys Banda, whom she referred to as "*Bafumahali*." Despite her critical condition, she was alert in her spirit and could sense what was happening in various geographic locations with clarity! Once more, we were in awe about how the Word we had received from the Lord on departure for Mongu was coming to pass in front of our very own eyes.

What happened this particular Sunday morning of October 4, 2015, made us sensitive to what the Holy Spirit was saying to us about how she was to be cared for until it was time for her to be with the Lord. It was an awesome experience to be ministered to so clearly by someone who was critically ill. This impacted most of the decisions we made and whatever we did for her in the ensuing two and half years until she went to be with the Lord on February 18, 2018.

I stood in awe of this Bo Ma-Matauka's God who had not only clearly spoken to us but had also confirmed His Word, an assurance that our God hears us when we call. He does what He says, and just as He promised to add days to our mother, giving her time to bless her generations, He did just that. What an awesome God we serve!

It dawned on me then that our mother's spiritual legacy was not only for her biological daughters, but also for other generations to come. God's faithfulness will be known by those who will believe, and they will in turn worship and honor His faithfulness. Our mother was honored with an inheritance for those who fear God. She was blessed with a long, fruitful life and went to be with her Lord at the ripe age of ninety-two years. God's goodness and mercy followed her as all the care and love she needed was available through her natural family, her daughters, the church family across denominations, the medical staff, and a faithful God who has remained our refuge and fortress.

Within the last two and half years of her life, great-grandchildren were born, and grandchildren came from faraway places to visit with her before she went to be with the Lord. She was a woman at peace as we continued to meet together, worship, and sing hymns and *Minembo* (praise songs) with her. My home in Roma, Lusaka, became a house of prayer, an altar to the Lord, and oh, how she delighted in all those moments as she joyfully sang and prayed along.

On Monday, October 12, 2015, midmorning, Bo Ma-Matauka was discharged from Lewanika General Hospital. The medical staff advised that we take her home to her village at Malengwa in Mongu district, where they would be sending a home-based caregiver once every fortnight to check on her and provide the support she needed. However, we took this matter to God in prayer as we desired the best for her. The three daughters who were on the ground at that moment (Matauka, Wamusheke, and Sibeso) requested a referral letter so she could receive better quality service in Lusaka, where we also resided. Lewanika General Hospital declined our request as they felt she was too old at eighty-nine years of age. We did take her to her home village but decided the same evening of Monday, October 12, 2015, to bring her with us to Lusaka for further medical attention.

This is a woman we felt deeply indebted to. We wanted her to receive the most excellent care in her hour of need the same way she had taken such good care of us. Against all odds, in spite of losing our father at a young age, Bo Ma-Matauka had stepped up to provide us with the care, support, and encouragement. Additionally, she had endeavored to educate all her daughters to the highest levels of education possible at a time when it was not the normal practice for the girl-child.

Before leaving Malengwa in Mongu that evening, we prayed for God's guidance for the long physical journey before us, the spiritual journey we were embarking on, and the medical interventions our mother needed to go through. We called St. John's, the Italian hospital in Lusaka, and made an appointment for her to be attended to immediately after we arrived the next morning. Our mother was quite physically spent after the long drive on poor roads. Her medical appointment was confirmed for the following morning, Tuesday, October 13, 2015.

We started off from our mother's home village shortly after dinner. We had barely covered a couple of kilometers along the Mongu-Lusaka Road when we noticed she was having some breathing problems. We stopped the car and prayed by the roadside for further guidance from the Lord whether to take her back to Lewanika General Hospital, where she had been discharged that same morning, or to proceed with her to Lusaka for help.

It was a miracle! As we prayed, she sat up with new strength, and her breathing normalized. The Holy Spirit clearly directed us to proceed to Lusaka. We continued driving in the night through Kaoma district, about 200 kilometers from Mongu.

After Kaoma, through Nkeyema district and on reaching the Kafue National Park, my mother, who had been lying down in the back seat of the car, sat upright and started to pray earnestly. We heard every single word she uttered. Her speech had not been that clear since she fell sick on September 29, 2015. She prayed through the Kafue National Park, sitting upright in the car until we reached Lusaka. It was early in the morning; therefore we drove straight to St. John's Hospital, where she was immediately attended to. We were overwhelmed by God's faithfulness as we prayed and thanked the Lord for the safe passage. We were well received at this hospital, and the medical examinations commenced immediately.

Praising God in Every Season

While under the care of one of the doctors, our mother, who had been sitting upright and had prayed throughout the journey from the Kafue National Park, suddenly grew faint and was immediately placed on oxygen. Soon we were advised to transfer her to the Coptic Hospital intensive care unit (ICU). We drove closely behind the ambulance, and by the time we got to Coptic Hospital, she no longer needed oxygen support. She was placed in the care of Dr. Beshara, who took very good care of our mother. We are forever grateful for his support and care for Mum for the two and half years he attended to her needs. At this first admission, we realized our mother was placed in the hands of a God-fearing senior medical doctor. When we thanked him for the way he received Mum and excellent care, he responded that he was simply an instrument in the hands of God! We were so encouraged and felt that God had directed us to the right hospital and to the right physician who were to provide quality care during her last days here on earth. Mum's steps were indeed ordered by her God.

Dr. Beshara took care of our mother from October 2015, during her regular reviews for a period of two years and five months. He was always there for Mum. Though she did not enjoy going to the hospital, her countenance always lifted once she met Dr. Beshara. He was God-sent to take care of our mother, and we are forever grateful for his support during our mother's last two years here on earth.

To further confirm the Word received about Mum on October 3, 2015, on Thursday, October 29, 2015, Mum's back, which was bent over after falling sick, suddenly straightened. This was a miracle as it occurred without the touch of a physician or physiotherapist attending to her back. This was the hand of her God, whom she believed in, loved, and ceaselessly worshiped despite her ill health.

The period between October 2015 and February 18, 2018, was one when my house in Roma became her residence. She lived with us until her death, turning my home into a house of continuous prayer, again confirming the Word given on October 3, 2015. All her four daughters were deeply impacted by God's love in one way or another. Our continuous prayers, the family, the members of the various congregations from Pentecostal Assemblies of God, the Baptist churches, United Church of Zambia, Seventh Day Adventist Church, the Catholic Church, and the independent church ministries all convened at my house to pray and worship the Lord and to offer encouragement. Christians of all walks came home and pronounced blessings over her four daughters.

During the second Sunday of January 2018, one of my Ugandan brothers in Christ, Dr. Nathan Bakyaita, who had recently relocated to Lusaka, Zambia, from Nairobi, Kenya, visited us. He had just been appointed as the World Health Organization (WHO) representative to Zambia. Dr. Nathan Bakyaita and his wife, Anne, were introduced to me in Nairobi through my prayer partner, Mrs. Christine Musisi, who is also Dr. Bakyaita's first cousin.

As soon as he entered my home, he said the atmosphere was different as he felt God's strong presence. God's manifest presence was felt because of the continuous prayers continually offered most of the day and night and with our mum residing there. It was indeed such a blessing and again a confirmation of the Word of God of Saturday, October 3, 2015. Dr. Nathan Bakyaita and his wife, Anne, joined these ongoing prayers. Our hearts were connected by the love of God so much that we, my mother's daughters, crowned Dr. Nathan Bakyaita as Mum's last-born son.

Dr. Nathan and Mrs. Anne Bakyaita.

Many other families from the African continent and beyond were also praying with us. Brethren from BEZA International Church in Ethiopia, Christ is the Answer Ministry (CITAM) in Nairobi (formerly Nairobi Pentecostal Church, Valley Road), Watoto Ministry in Kampala Uganda (formerly Kampala Pentecostal Church), and Hatfield Christian Church in Pretoria, South Africa. The messages from all these locations were that though they had not met Bo Ma-Matauka in person, they felt a strong bond with her in the spirit and sent their blessings to us, her daughters, and all other family members. Prayers were also offered from beyond the African continent to the glory of God. It was indeed overwhelming just seeing how God was connecting His big church family through the illness of His maidservant, our mother.

Bo Ma-Matauka's Homegoing Send-off: It Was One Glorious Day!

The day Mum went to be with the Lord, Sunday, February 18, 2018, will go into our annals as a remembrance day. We were witnesses of the glory of the Lord coming down. Though unplanned, somehow, we were all gathered, her children, grandchildren, both biological and spiritual, and some other Christians from various churches in Lusaka who just promptly gathered at my place to visit with her. We had eaten together and sung gospel songs and hymns, praising and worshiping joyfully together. It had not been like that for some time. We prayed, and Dr. Nathan Bakyaita recited her favorite scripture passage, Psalm 23. We had not informed him that it was her favorite psalm! We always joked that if she were given a chance to provide the scripture on the tombstone for all her children, it would have been Psalm 23 in Silozi or English. We also joked that whoever would go next among us should know what would be engraved on their tombstone.

On this special day, we prayed the Lord's prayer together, laughed, and danced. She was joy-filled, smiling and witnessing all that was happening around her and with an unusual glow, a bright countenance on her face. She had not exuded that bright look on her face for a while.

Shortly after 4:00 p.m., the guests started leaving the house, and so did two of her daughters and the grandchildren present in Lusaka. As soon as the visitors dispersed, the situation suddenly changed. Bo Ma-Matauka became breathless, and within fifteen minutes, she departed this world forever. She went to be with her maker, and we all knew she was ready to meet Him! Her eldest daughter was just entering the main gate to her residence on the other side of Lusaka city when I called to inform her that Mum had left us. She mentioned she had just been narrating to her neighbors what a marvelous day we'd had with Mum. What a homegoing send-off that February 18, 2018, was for my mother! She had "fought a good fight, finished the race, and kept the Faith" (2 Timothy 4:7).

Bo Ma-Matauka's Burial

Bo Ma-Matauka's homegoing send-off.

Our mother demonstrated her faith throughout her long life from the time we were young to the day she went to be with her God. The testimonies from Mongu by some of her spiritual sons, daughters, and grandchildren were uplifting. They told accolades of how she took care of them and impacted their lives. They had only one request in her honor, that her remains be taken back to Malengwa in Mongu for burial for a befitting send-off. They were so glad when we concluded that according to her wish, she was to be buried next to her late parents and brother. The very place where she had established the Malengwa Community Church on the model of

Sefula Transformational Center. The UCZ Bishop for the Western Presbytery had also graciously recommended that she be buried either at Sefula, PEMS, or Mabumbu PEMS, which befitted the men and women who had faithfully served God to such magnitude. We, however, informed him that Bo Ma-Matauka's wish was to be buried in Malengwa, and thus, he released us and gave us his blessing.

When we arrived with the hearse and funeral convoy escorting her remains from Lusaka, multitudes were waiting just before entry into Mongu town along the Lusaka-Mongu Road. The Christians from various denominations in Mongu monitored our travel from Lusaka to Mongu, and as we approached Mongu, they all gathered by the roadside to receive her body on February 20, 2018. We found people in buses and vehicles waiting to receive her remains and escort her to Mukwamalundu village/Malengwa royal village, where she had established her last home and planted the church. Many came forth to pay their last respects to this woman of God who had touched their lives powerfully.

Her send-off ceremony was conducted by one of her spiritual grandsons, Reverend Chisha, who hailed from the Northern Province of Zambia. He had become a committed member of this church that Mum had established. He served as a deacon and then proceeded to further training to become a reverend. He considered Bo Ma-Matauka as his grandmother as she had received him and taken him in like her own long-lost son. Their relationship has extended to us, her children, and we see him as one of the members of the family. Reverend Chisha considered it a privilege to be the lead reverend in this send-off ceremony.

Speakers, one after another, stood up to share what this old African mama, Bo Ma, Ima, Bo Ma-Matauka, had done for them. The church members gave tributes and shared testimonies of how the church had been constructed, managed, and continued to grow through her support. Several shared how impactful her life was during the construction of the church; she would not go to her house for lunch but chose to stay behind to ensure all was going well and to monitor the progress of the house of God. She had treasured and was fully committed to this project that the Lord, the Holy Spirit, had urged her to construct to the glory of His name.

CHAPTER 9

MY MOTHER'S BLESSING

Spiritual Blessings through Mum on Her Sickbed

"The LORD will strengthen him on his bed of illness; You will sustain him on his sickbed" (Psalm 41:3 KJV).

Bo Ma-Matauka was on her sickbed from October2015 until February 2018, and even then, she gave us something that nobody else could give, spiritual blessings that have remained more meaningful to us than any natural blessings, for they have continued to deepen our faith in God. From her, we were bequeathed a spiritual inheritance, promises of God and learnings throughout the season of her illness, helping us to become more Christ-like and to live in the abundance that God has provided, being fully satisfied in Him. The following ten blessings were proclaimed over us, and we are appropriating them for ourselves, particularly considering the Word we received from the Lord on October 3, 2015.

1. The Blessing of Abiding in God's Presence

During Mum's illness, we focused day and night on the Lord and all that matters to God in this life. And therefore, we can affirm we received the blessing in Psalm 91. I know it is what Bo Ma-Matauka would want the world to know, that those who stay focused on the Most High God, focused on who He is and what He says in His Word, will perceive this natural world through the lens of heaven, being daily reminded that God's promises are sure. We were reminded daily that despite Mum's illness, we were not alone; God was with us and would never leave us. What a comfort that was! We prayed and appropriated Psalm 91 for ourselves, and we experienced God's presence, peace, and amazing love through the period of adversity.

> Those who live in the shelter of the Most High will find rest in the shadow of the Almighty. This I declare about the Lord; He alone is my refuge, my place of safety; He is my God, and I trust Him for He will rescue you from every trap and protect you from deadly disease. He will cover you with His feathers. He will shelter you with His wings. His faithful promises are your armor and protection. Do not be afraid of the terrors of the night, nor that arrow that flies in the day. Do not dread the disease that stalks the darkness, nor the disaster that strikes at midday. Though a thousand fall at your side, though ten thousand are dying around you, these evils will not touch you. (Psalm 91:1–7 NLT)

As this promise was spoken in our lives, we realized that in every situation, our focus was to be on the Lord. Whether facing sickness or other life challenges, our first point of call must be the Lord. We are to seek Him before taking any other action or seeking help from elsewhere.

2. The Blessing of Spending Time in God's Word

A treasure is found in being thoroughly drenched and refreshed by abiding in God's presence. It may be as simple as picking up the Bible, reading a verse or a portion of scripture, meditating on it, thanking God for His Word, and listening to what He might have to say. We experienced the joy of spending time in God's presence and His Word during the last two and half years of our mother's life here on earth. We were filled with such peace daily as we spent most of our time in Worship. We could feel God's manifest presence, and indeed we can declare, "I have seen you in the sanctuary and gazed upon your power and glory. Your unfailing love is better than life itself. How I praise you! I will praise you as long as I live lifting up my hands to you in prayer. You satisfy me more than the richest feast. I will praise you with songs of joy" (Psalm 63:2–5 NLT).

3. The Blessing of Sharing the Gospel

Our commitment to the cause and urgency of sharing the gospel of the kingdom was rekindled in all those who visited Mum. We became more aware of the need to continue the spiritual legacy by inviting people to come to Jesus for life-giving water. Bo Ma-Matauka's voice still rings out, "Share the gospel, send the light, be missionaries to the lost, get involved as devoted laborers in His vineyard, proclaim his word in the marketplace and wherever an opportunity presents itself."

> Is anyone thirsty? Come and drink even if you have no money! Come, take your choice of wine or milk, it's all free! Why spend your money on food that does you no good? Listen to me, and you will eat what is good. You will enjoy the finest food, come to me with your ears wide open. Listen, and you will

find life. I will make an everlasting covenant with you. I will give you all the unfailing love I promised to David. (Isaiah 55:1–3 NLT).

4. The Blessing of the Holy Spirit

There was a heavy manifest presence of the Holy Spirit, and as we sensed His overflow in our lives, we lived a life of sustained blessings, with frequent visitations, prayers offered by different Christians from across the faith divide. "On the last day, the climax of the festival, Jesus stood and shouted to the crowds, 'Anyone who is thirsty may come to me! Anyone who believes in me may come and drink! For the Scriptures declare, 'Rivers of living water will flow from his heart'" (John 7:37–39 NLT).

When Jesus spoke of "living water," He was referring to the Holy Spirit, who would be available to everyone who believes in Him. Through the season of our mother's illness, we got to value spiritual blessings over natural blessings and realized that relationships with fellow believers are more satisfying than material benefits.

5. The Blessing of Growing in Faith

We grew in faith then as young people, and we have continued to grow in faith whenever the Holy Spirit brings to remembrance our mother's legacy. We received the spiritual gift of faith and extraordinary confidence in God's promises, power, and presence.

> I am writing to you who share the same precious faith we have. This faith was given to you because of the justice and fairness of Jesus Christ, our God and Savior. May God give you more and more grace and peace as you grow in your knowledge of God and Jesus our Lord. (2 Peter 1:1b–2 NLT)

We realized that the joy and peace our mother had in her last days here on earth was based on her faith and the hope she had in her Redeemer, for the fruit of the Spirit includes love, joy, and peace.

6. Multiple Spiritual Blessings in Christ

There are spiritual blessings in Christ given by grace through faith, as detailed in Ephesians 1:3–14, that are indescribable and incomprehensible in the natural view of things. They include riches in glory, the presence of God, and our eternal home. These are the things that "No eye has seen, no ear has heard, and no mind has imagined what God has prepared for those who love him" (1 Corinthians 2:9 NLT). This is the guaranteed inheritance available to every believer in Christ. This blessing made us realize how important it is to set our hearts to worship and praise God. As believers worship, God makes Himself known more and more and reveals deeper things that we cannot comprehend in the natural. What a blessing it is to worship the maker of heaven and earth!

7. The Blessing of Restoration

We experienced so much joy in just taking time to remember what Bo Ma-Matauka taught us in our growing-up years. We nursed her as an invalid for two years and five months, yet never found it a strain or a burden; rather, it was an honor to serve our late mom. The joy of the Lord was our strength, and we were completely strengthened and healed both spiritually and physically as promised in His Word, "by his wounds you have been healed" (1 Peter 2:24c) and "He took up our infirmities and bore our diseases" (Matthew 8:17). Both our spiritual and physical healing is provided for by the suffering of Christ and the power of His resurrection. Hallelujah!

8. The Blessing of Calling on God in Prayer

God continually revealed so much to us about our mother's life and us through the last two years and five months of her life here on earth. We understood that when we call on the Lord in prayer, God answers and reveals to us His mysteries and purposes. "Call to me and I will answer you and tell you great and unsearchable things you do not know" (Jeremiah 33:3).

Though we may not always understand what God is doing behind the scenes, He invites us to call unto Him and trust Him anyway. He promises to show us great and mighty things, His healing, peace, and truth, as He is constantly at work to rebuild and restore in mercy and loving kindness. We are always to remember that the source of all these blessings is the person of Jesus Christ so our focus is not on these good gifts, but on the giver.

9. The Blessing of a Discerning Spirit

During this same period, we were blessed with the spirit of discernment and faith to understand the blessings we have in Christ, that our faith may become effectual, perfected with wisdom, knowledge, understanding, and love as described in Philemon 1:6, to enable others to partake of the same faith as they observe our good deeds toward others. In so doing, that all might acknowledge this faith to be genuine and efficacious. It is our persistent prayer that "may we demonstrate faith" (Titus 1:1), "work our salvation with trembling and love" (Galatians 5:6), and "serve and demonstrate good works" (James 2:18).

10. The Blessing of Being Unconditionally Loved

We were and continue being saturated with God's unconditional love and immutable blessings as described in Isaiah 54. That the Lord's unconditional promise is to extend his unconditional love to us, for with everlasting kindness, He will have mercy on us, and His covenant of peace with us shall not be removed. Isaiah 54:10 (NLT) reads, "'For the mountains may move and the hills disappear, but even then, my faithful love for you will remain. My covenant of blessing will never be broken,' says the Lord, who has mercy on you." This way, we shall have the privilege of extending God's territory, sharing the gospel, and experiencing the joy of the Lord as we walk along life's journey until the day when we will meet our maker in heaven.

CHAPTER 10

THE GENERATIONAL IMPACT

Tributes to Bo Ma-Matauka by Her Children and Grandchildren

"We will not hide these truths from our children; we will tell the next generation about the glorious deeds of the Lord, about his power and his mighty wonders. For he issued his laws to Jacob; he gave his instructions to Israel. He commanded our ancestors to teach them to their children, so the next generation might know them—even the children not yet born—and they in turn will teach their own children. So, each generation should set its hope anew on God, not forgetting his glorious miracles and obeying his commands" (Psalm 78:4–7 NLT).

Bo Ma-Matauka left behind many who remember her as a servant, transformational leader, and church planter who boldly told the next generation about the Lord Jesus Christ. She was a gifted organizer who served her generation well, with a knack for bringing people together and influencing them toward a noble cause. By the time of her departure, she had left her four daughters who had a solid faith foundation, trusting in the Lord Jesus Christ. We continually remember God's wondrous deeds in our lives because through her deliberate actions, we learned to meditate on the Word of God, praying through the power of the Holy Spirit and keeping His commands through His enabling grace.

A Tribute by Rose Kashembe Sakala, Third Daughter

Bo Rose Kashembe, third daughter of Bo Ma-Matauka.

Rose Kashembe Sakala was the daughter firmly held by the hand by Bo Ma-Matauka when she encountered the lion in the African savannah. She fondly remembers her mother had the following to say.

Our mother was very inspiring and motivating. I remember when my father died, I thought that was the end of the world for my family. I was quite young, and never had I imagined that my father would one day be taken from our lives. In that dark season of my life, my mother's disposition changed all that. A very perceptive, sharp-minded woman, she was quick to notice this negative vibe, and I vividly recall her setting the tone for our future with the words, "Your father passed on too early in your lives, and God will help me fill that gap going forward." Her strong resolve and determination were so convincing that they inspired hope in us all. We were no longer afraid. She repositioned herself, redefined her roles, and gracefully played multiple roles as a model Christian, diligent breadwinner, teacher, mentor, and counselor. She never gave up or allowed challenging circumstances to deter her. She persevered and was always full of hope that the Lord our God would always show her the way. This is one of the seeds she firmly planted in all of us, her children. I am eternally grateful to have been raised by such a remarkable African mama.

A Tribute by Magodi Muchiwa Sakala, Grandson

Magodi Muchiwa Sakala.

Magodi is the firstborn son to the third daughter, Rose Kashembe Sakala, and has the following to say.

> I hold very fond memories of my grandmother, Bo Ma-Matauka; Mongu, her village; and the many people who would always be coming in and out of her home. They would be of every cadre, making impromptu visits, and yet they would be graciously welcomed. My grandmother was highly respected in the community, and she had excellent interpersonal and communication skills. Whenever my family went to visit with her, I would be struck by the evident order of things; she was highly organized. She valued a clean environment, and I observed her deliberateness in observing hygiene practices in her home and the surrounding area. My grandmother loved her God with all her heart and would often work

while humming a tune, a hymn, or a psalm or singing a song. A specific visit I made in 2010 remains etched in my memory when the new Malengwa community church she had planted was under construction. She was fully engaged in the process and inspired the builders and all those involved beautifully. She also paid keen attention to my academic progress and offered me encouragement to keep pursuing my education. I think continuous learning is one aspect that seems to have rubbed on all of us in the family, thanks to my incredible African grandma.

A Tribute by Lucy Amanda Wabei Lisulo, Granddaughter

Lucy Amanda Wabei Lisulo.

Lucy is the daughter to the fourth daughter, Sibeso Mukoboto Luswata, the baby who was strapped on Bo Ma Matauka's back the day she encountered the lion in the African savannah and the author of this book. Lucy had the following to say.

My fond name for my grandma was *Kuku*, meaning "grandparent" in Lozi language. I was always warmly welcomed and loved in my grandma's home. Bo Ma-Matauka never turned down an opportunity to receive people into her space; all were welcome, cared for, and made to feel valued consistently through the years.

Bo Ma-Matauka, my grandmother, was very protective of me and showed this through her love and care. She intentionally created quality time to connect with me, which filled me with a sense of belonging. She was a joyful soul, full of cheer, often singing out loud as she carried on with her daily business.

Kuku loved the Word of God and exhibited childlike faith. I watched her invest time in preparing weekly quizzes for the various groups in church to compete in during the weekly Bible study sessions at the church she had planted. She was devoted to serving the church daily throughout the week, not only on Sundays. Since there was always something to be done, she offered her time and energy to ensure it was done well. She organized for prayer-fellowship meetings, Bible study sessions, Bible fun quiz time, choir practice, and cleaning of the church. Kuku also planned for the Sunday services in Lozi language, received visitors, and engaged in community visits to those in need. I always felt at ease around Grandma, comforted by her presence, and this made me treasure being in the presence of the Lord.

Kuku loved her family, and her home had an atmosphere of love and joy. She had such a loving sibling relationship with her brother. They would sit to chat together, joke, break out in mirthful laughter, and sing together. They were friends in such a beautiful way, something I long to see in sibling relationships across the family. She was a peacemaker who pursued peace with all people and, in this way, pointed the rest of the family to Christ as our model. Innumerable blessings have been sourced from her and continue to be passed down from generation to generation because of her faithfulness to God. When my grandmother died, I was devastated and found relief in the following tribute, which I wrote and shared on the day her body was laid to rest.

Dear Kuku,

You were truly treasured and loved by us all. You gave love, support and comfort to all who crossed paths with You. I was privileged enough to have had a relationship with You, and shared many special moments that allowed me to feel loved, and I will forever cherish those moments! You were a pillar of strength in Your community, an active Kingdom builder, and a faithful servant of the Most High God! You lived a life that was full and with Purpose! Immaculate in Your ways, You were a Mother, a Grandmother, and a Great-Grandmother to many, many of whom You taught the ways of life and imparted Your Gracious and Kind nature. And now that God has taken You under his wing, May You sing and dance with the Angels! And until we meet again, we Love You dearly and we will miss You Greatly! May You Rest In Eternal Peace.

Lots of Love, Lucy.

Lucy's gold-framed tribute to her grandmother.

A Tribute by Dr. Sibeso Mukoboto Luswata

Dr. Sibeso Luswata.

Sibeso was the fourth-born daughter of Bo Ma-Matauka. Sibeso was the baby strapped on her mother's back when they encountered the lion in the African savannah forest. The conversation that shaped Sibeso's life took place just after her father died, and she relates it as follows.

My mother, Bo Ma-Matauka, was in deep grief, mourning losing the love of her life. She was surrounded by relatives and friends who had come to console her. Only that she happened to be a mother to girls only! This was at a time when society neither held women in high regard nor considered them worthy of an education. My eyes as a nine-year-old child, bewildered by all that was happening around me, were on her when she looked up and boldly stated that her God would provide for her daughters. Her response changed my life forever, following a question from them about what she was planning to do with her daughters upon the passing on of the head of the household.

My deceased father was considered well-off, and he did take very good care of his family. In her response, my mother acknowledged the role our father had played as a model head of the household. However, she told those in her hearing that as much as she appreciated all he had done for us, she knew who the real provider was. Her God, Jehovah Jireh, was her provider, and He would provide for her family. The way she said that is what got my attention, with a deep conviction and confident trust, leaving me yearning to know her God in the same way for myself. If my grieving mother, whom I had seen broken from the pain of loss could respond this way, then her God must become my God too. I surrendered to my mother's Jesus at the tender age of nine years.

My Parents' Dream

My parents had dreams for us, their daughters, despite them not having done gender studies. Our mother had studied her scriptures well and knew of situations where her God had turned and changed systems for the sake of the girl-child. She understood from her study of the Word about Caleb's daughter who had received more than was expected of a girl-child in Joshua 15:13–19 and Joshua 17:3–6.

And Caleb said, "I will give my daughter Aksah in marriage to the man who attacks and captures

Kiriath Sepher." Othniel son of Kenaz, Caleb's brother, took it; so, Caleb gave his daughter Aksah to him in marriage. One day when she came to Othniel, she urged him to ask her father for a field. When she got off her donkey, Caleb asked her, "What can I do for you?" She replied, "Do me a special favor. Since you have given me land in the Negev, give me also springs of water." So Caleb gave her the upper and lower springs. (Joshua 16:16–19)

Caleb's daughter, Aksah, simply made a request, and it was granted. Through prayer, she received the double portion she had requested.

Now Zelophehad son of Hepher, the son of Gilead, the son of Makir, the son of Manasseh, had no sons but only daughters, whose names were Mahlah, Noah, Hoglah, Milkah, and Tirzah. They went to Eleazar the priest, Joshua son of Nun, and the leaders and said, "The Lord commanded Moses to give us an inheritance among our relatives." So Joshua gave them an inheritance along with the brothers of their father, according to the Lord's command. Manasseh's share consisted of ten tracts of land besides Gilead and Bashan east of the Jordan, because the daughters of the tribe of Manasseh received an inheritance among the sons. The land of Gilead belonged to the rest of the descendants of Manasseh. (Joshua 17:3–6)

From her Bible study, Bo Ma-Matauka understood the narrative about the five daughters of the posterity of Hepher. Even though they were all women, they appealed to the land appraisers, and each was endowed with an inheritance in land. These experiences of real women in the Bible fascinated her greatly.

The daughters of Zelophehad son of Hepher, the son of Gilead, the son of Makir, the son of Manasseh, belonged to the clans of Manasseh son of Joseph. The names of the daughters were Mahlah, Noah, Hoglah, Milkah and Tirzah. They came forward and stood before Moses, Eleazar the priest, the leaders, and the whole assembly at the entrance to the tent of meeting and said, "Our father died in the wilderness. He was not among Korah's followers, who banded together against the Lord, but he died for his own sin and left no sons. Why should our father's name disappear from his clan because he had no son? Give us property among our father's relatives." So Moses brought their case before the Lord, and the Lord said to him, "What Zelophehad's daughters are saying is right. You must certainly give them property as an inheritance among their father's relatives and give their father's inheritance to them. (Numbers 27:1–7)

These five daughters simply brought their inheritance claim before the Lord through Moses and were granted land along with their father's male relatives. Bo Ma-Matauka's faith in God's infallible Word caused her to believe that one day her daughters would take their place in the land and make their mark in the marketplace, not only at the national level but at a global stage. She was confident about what the Lord had promised to her and Dad, alongside what the scriptures affirmed could happen.

Bo Ma-Matauka sent off my elder sister, Rose Kashembe Sakala, and me, Sibeso Mukoboto Luswata, to the same mission schools for primary and secondary education that had grown her faith and built her character to follow Jesus diligently. This deliberate move made us grow in our faith in the two PEMS schools of *Mabumbu* and *Sefula*. These institutions followed the same values and had the same practices she had taught us in the home, of early morning devotions, school assemblies or prayers, evening devotions in the dormitories, and missionary influence in the classes throughout the day. The discipline and culture continued to shape our lives, and we excelled in our studies.

I was able to compete at a national level, entered university on my first attempt, and was awarded full bursaries through all my studies. My mother did not have to worry about paying for my tuition, boarding, or school requirements. With her encouragement that I could make my claim through prayer like Caleb's daughter and the five daughters of Zelophehad, I soldiered on. I later learned of a call for African girls to apply for the AFRGRAD scholarship in the United States, which again provided a full bursary, including tuition, textbooks, accommodation, warm clothing, summer school courses, and whatever else was required to complete the required post-graduate program. I applied by faith, received a high score, and was admitted for graduate studies for a master's that would also gain me entry into a doctorate program. My mother insisted that we pray at every stage of the process, entrusting all we needed or planned at God's feet so they could be established. She would point us to scriptures such as, "Don't worry about anything; instead, pray about everything. Tell God what you need and thank Him for all He has done" (Philippians 4:6) and "Commit your actions to the Lord, and your plans will succeed" (Proverbs 16:3).

Through her prayers, which started when we were very young, through the time my dad was still alive and long after his demise, and into the phase when she was raising girls, I soon became Dr. Sibeso Mukoboto Luswata, EdD (Doctor of Education). I have served as a notable and prominent educator, both in Africa and globally, a social transformer, and a champion for children's rights. I am serving as an international consultant and UN expert on mission and a mentor for the Young African Thinkers as I write this book. I have also been privileged to serve as an expert reviewer for the Continental Education Strategy for Africa (CESA 2025).

Most notably, I was chief of education for the largest UNICEF-supported program in Eastern and Southern Africa. Dr. Luswata spearheaded various programs that focused on the promotion and development of education in several African countries, among them Ethiopia, South Sudan, South Africa, Kenya, Uganda, Malawi, Botswana, Namibia, and Zimbabwe, with considerable success. I have grown into a professional and prolific writer of substance and written material on areas such as early childhood development, curriculum design and development, educational leadership, education management development, gender into and through education, monitoring and evaluation, education in emergencies, and various Christian writings. I have also been engaged in designing systems such as Rapid Assessment of Learning Spaces (RALS), Education Management Systems (EMIS), curriculum from early childhood through tertiary education, vocational education, and science, math, and technology (STEM).

I owe my successes on the professional and corporate scene to God and my incredible African mother. The achievement I consider my greatest is that I am a born-again Christian who has and continues to participate in, facilitate, and promote several Christian movements, notably, the Africa Arise movement and Young African Thinkers. I am a minister-at-large for the Africa Arise movement, which is about redeeming nations in righteousness. This is where the children and young people call me "Mama Africa." What a privilege to serve the now and next generation! I am also a marketplace motivator for Possessing the Land and reaching unreached peoples and nations, which is the mandate for Northmead Assembly of God Church in Lusaka, Zambia, where I serve as a deaconess responsible for quality assurance.

Bo Ma-Matauka's unwavering commitment to living God's purpose for her life became my passion too as I pursue investment in the protection of children and young people to extend God's kingdom. I owe it all to my remarkable African mama!

CHAPTER 11

BO MA-MATAUKA POSTERITY

A Global Impact

Like Daniel, who was preserved in the lions' den and rose to serve the nation through many eras of leadership, Dr. Sibeso Luswata was preserved from a lion encounter along with her sister, Rose Kashembe Sakala, and their late mother, Bo Ma-Matauka, to serve her generation in the continent of Africa. Some of the highlights from Dr. Luswata's work in some select African countries include among others:

South Africa: Education Transformation

Dr. Luswata, one of Bo Ma-Matauka's daughters, became the first education officer of the newly established UNICEF office after the dismantling of official apartheid in South Africa in 1994. The first major task was to transform the education system as a key to transforming society. Education had been used to perpetuate apartheid; therefore, the new government decided to use education to reverse and transform the post-apartheid South African society. Dr. Luswata conceptualized a highly innovative program on education management development, curriculum for transformations, and integrated early childhood development. She conceptualized a highly innovative program on techno-girls, which has been evaluated globally and adopted by UN Women and UNESCO in promoting math, science, and technology for girls in Africa. This program has proven to be highly successful in South Africa, Ghana, Kenya, and many other AU member countries in promoting quality education and STEM through techno-girls.

Uganda

Dr. Luswata supported the conceptualization of a highly successful program on early literacy for African languages and the application of appreciative inquiry in community-based early childhood development. She led the process for the strategy formulation for universal primary education and universal secondary education. From 1995 to 2000, UNICEF was the lead technical support organization. Dr. Luswata was then the head of education in Uganda, spearheading some of the work on education financing, including the first-ever sector-wide approach in Eastern and Southern Africa. She provided the lead in inclusive education and the education of marginalized groups in Uganda through complementary and alternative approaches to education. One of the most successful approaches was that through Alternative Basic Education for Karamoja (ABEK), which methodology was adopted for Tanzania, Ethiopia, and most of the Horn of African countries to promote universal basic education. These ideas also spread to parts of Southern Africa to promote community schools, which were adopted in various forms in Malawi and Zambia to promote universal primary and secondary education. As head of UNICEF Education in Uganda, she conceptualized and promoted the Girls' Education Movement (GEM) and promoted it through the African heads of state and government to take to the UN General Assembly. This was adopted and formed the core of the African Girls' Education Initiative (AGEI), which eventually was adopted by the UN and still runs as UN Girls' Education Initiative (UNGEI). From the GEM emerged the Boys Education Movement (BEM) for Lesotho (cattle herders) and parts of Botswana, where some boys were disadvantaged.

South Sudan

From 2005 through September 2009, Dr. Luswata worked as chief of education for UNICEF, leading the "Go To School Initiative in South Sudan." After twenty-one years of conflict and the signing of the comprehensive peace agreement in Naivasha, Kenya, on January 9, 2005, as sector lead for education, Dr. Luswata also acted as the lead international partner to the ministry of education, science, and technology in all matters relating to education in South Sudan. The program was positively evaluated in 2009 and recorded as one of the most successful "Education in Emergencies" programs globally.

Ethiopia

Dr. Luswata served with UNICEF before her retirement on March 31, 2014, as chief of education, addressing developing regional states and other more developed regions on a humanitarian, recovery, and development continuum. Her mother's investment in her Christian walk has seen her contribute to numerous technical publications. Of special interest to this publication are the four of the *Africa Arise* series, published and printed by Asaph Office Publications (AOP) book division in Nairobi, Kenya, including the following titles:

- Africa Arise, Series 1, 2011: *The Kingdom of God Will Never Be Shaken*

- Africa Arise, Series 2, 2013: *This Is the Season of Jubilee! Africa Arise and Redeem the Nations in Righteousness*
- Africa Arise, Series 3, 2014: *Walking in Destiny and Purpose*
- Africa Arise Series 4, Zambia Chapter, 2016: *Embracing Our Destiny: Redeeming Zambia in Righteousness—Africa's Tithe*

This impact upon nations by Bo Ma-Matauka's offspring occurred, fueled by a cover of our late father's dreams and the ceaseless prayers made by our remarkable mother, Bo Ma-Matauka. Her daughters have continued to diligently work and serve across the nations as unto the Lord.

> Work willingly at whatever you do, as though you were working for the Lord rather than for people. Remember that the Lord will give you an inheritance as your reward, and that the Master you are serving is Christ. (Colossians 3:23–24 NLT)

AFTERWORD

A Mother's Honor

Dear reader, you can be assured that the blessings you are storing your family and community will not only come over your own seed, but they will also outlive you and get passed on to the next generation. It is therefore not in vain that you are storing up prayer, offering praise to God, singing psalms, worshiping the Lord, dwelling in His presence, and loving God passionately. For your sake, God will remember and be faithful to take care of your next, the next, and the next generation, just like He did for the sake of His servants, Abraham, David, and Jacob.

> For the sake of my servant Jacob, and Israel my chosen, I call you by your name, I name you, though you do not know me. (Isaiah 45:4 ESV)

> For I will defend this city to save it for My own sake and for My servant David's sake. (2 Kings 19:34)

True spiritual legacy begins the moment we acknowledge and believe in what God left in us and for us. This legacy holds the keys to unlock the power to live an overcoming life, release answers, and find solutions that overcome the present or arising challenges. It makes the unseen seen and the impossible possible.

Bo Ma-Matauka was a remarkable African mother who understood that the development of the heart and spirit of a man has real lasting value. She was deliberate in investing her best in shaping who her children became, boldly shared her faith, and pointed people to what matters the most through living for posterity. In step with Bo Ma-Matauka's footprints, it is our time to live for posterity, establishing a legacy of faith, hope, and love that will outlive us.

Collage with Bo Ma-Matauka surrounded by her siblings, children, grandchildren, and great-grandchildren.

SELECTED BIBLIOGRAPHY

Arnot, F. S. *From Natal to the Upper Zambezi: First Year Among the Barotse*. Glasgow: Mission, 1883.

—. *Garenganze: or, Seven Years Pioneer Mission Work in Central Africa*. London: Hawkins, 1889.

—. *Missionary Travels in Central Africa*. London: Holness, 1914.

Interviews and conversations with family members: Bo Matauka Njebele, firstborn daughter; Mrs. Monde Sikatana, sister-in-law; Bo Wamusheke Njebele, second-born daughter; Bo Rose Kashembe Sakala, third-born daughter; Magodi Muchiwa Sakala, grandson; and Lucy Amanda Wabei Lisulo, granddaughter.

McDonald F. W. *The Story of Mashonaland and The Missionary Pioneers*. London: Wesleyan Mission House, 1893.

Mackintosh, C. W. *Coillard of the Zambesi*. London: Unwin, 1907.

Macmillan, H. *An African Trading Empire: The Story of Susman Borthers and Wulfsohn, 1901–2005*. London: I B Tauris & Co Ltd, 2005.

Rae, W. F. *George Westbeech and the Barotseland missionaries 1878–1888*. Salisbury: Central Africa Historical Association, 1968.

Spindler, Marc R. F. Coillard, *On the Threshold of Central Africa: A Record of Twenty Years' Pioneering among the Barotsi of the Upper Zambesi* (1897; French, *Sur le Haut-Zambèze*, 1898). Édouard

Fabre, *La vie d'un missionnaire français: François Coillard*, 1834–1904 (1922); Catherine Winkworth Mackintosh, *Coillard of the Zambesi: The Lives of François and Christina Coillard, of the Paris Missionary Society, in South and Central Africa*, 1858–1904 (1907).

Endorsement by Christine Musisi, resident representative of UNDP Tanzania (2019–2023) and founder, ONGOZA Africa!

Excerpt from the Foreword

This book you are reading, *Living for Posterity—My Remarkable African Mother: Bo Wabei Lisulo a.k.a. Bo Ma-Matauka,* has inspired me immensely. It has given me a clear understanding of the importance of intergenerational impact- that whatever we do in this generation is a seed sown to multiply in future generations. We therefore must plant good seeds in good soil.

It has taught me that a deep love for God and His Word propels one into service to others with effortless, genuine love. It drives purpose, shapes one's dreams, and empowers one with energy and resources to serve the most vulnerable, while influencing decisions that affect their lives.

I have also learned that God's miracles are still alive in our days! The way he shut the mouths of lions in the story of Daniel in Babylon is the same way he shut the mouth of the lion when Bo Wabei Lisulo encountered it in the rolling hills of Zambia, with my friend Sibeso as a child strapped on her back! The Lord spared His daughters for a great purpose. Sibeso, in her capacity as chief of education in UNICEF and expert in other platforms, has shaped education policies and practices globally and particularly in Africa. As a Christian minister, she has diligently mentored the Young African Thinkers in Ethiopia, Zambia, and Kenya. She has touched numerous lives with her love and generosity. She has also taught me what it means to be a true servant and friend of God.

Printed in the United States
by Baker & Taylor Publisher Services